REFERENCES TO SALVADOR DALÍ MAKE ME HOT

AND OTHER PLAYS

REFERENCES TO SALVADOR DALÍ MAKE ME HOT

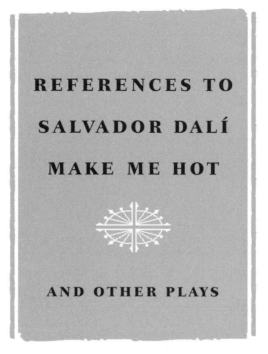

AND OTHER PLAYS

JOSÉ RIVERA

THEATRE COMMUNICATIONS GROUP
NEW YORK
2003

References to Salvador Dalí Make Me Hot and Other Plays is published by
Theatre Communications Group, Inc., 520 Eighth Avenue, 24th Floor,
New York, NY 10018-4156.

This publication is made possible in part with public funds from
the New York State Council on the Arts, a State Agency.

TCG books are exclusively distributed to the book trade by Consortium Book
Sales and Distribution, 1045 Westgate Dr., St. Paul, MN 55114.

LIBRARY OF CONGRESS CATALOGING-IN-PUBLICATION DATA
Rivera, José, 1955–
References to Salvador Dalí make me hot and other plays / by José
Rivera—1st ed.
p. cm.
ISBN 1-55936-212-X (alk.paper)
I. Title: References to Salvador Dalí make me hot. II Title.
PS3568.I8294 R44 2002
812'.54—dc21
2002007441

Book design and typography by Lisa Govan
Cover design by Kitty Suen
Cover photo "La Luna, 1989" is by Luis González Palma

First edition, May 2003

For Adena and Teo

Art is the conversation between lovers.
Art offers an opening for the heart.
True art makes the divine silence in the soul
Break into applause.

Art is, at last, the knowledge of
Where we are standing—
Where we are standing
In this Wonderland
When we rip off all our clothes . . .

—**HAFIZ**

☙ CONTENTS ❧

REFERENCES TO
SALVADOR DALÍ
MAKE ME HOT

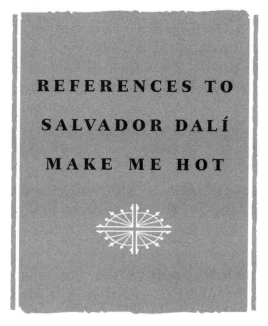

This play is dedicated to my soldier-brothers:
Julio, Charlie, Tony and Hector

SPECIAL THANKS TO

Julia Edwards, Jo Bonney, John Ortiz, Camilia Sanes, Jeff Storer, Jessica Hecht, Jerry Patch, John Dias, Mervin P. Antonio, Zannie Voss, Michele Vazquez, Maricela Ochoa, Iona Brindle, Ruth Livier, Oscar Arguello, Rachel Malkenhorst, Wendy Johnson, Jesus Mendoza, Stefan Olmsted, Adam Rosenblatt, Dana Parker Bennison, Imoh Ime Essien, Adam Saunders, Joel McCauley Jr., Chris Schussler, Laura K. Lewis, Julio Monge, Tony Torn, Danyon Davis, Carlo Alban, Timothy Huang, Shirley Fishman, Richard Coca, Sol Castillo, Sue Karutz, John Iacovelli, Doc Ballard, Nephelie Andonyadis and Megan Monaghan

References to Salvador Dalí Make Me Hot was developed with the assistance of the Mark Taper Forum (Gordon Davidson, Artistic Director), the Ensemble Studio Theatre West (Garrett Brown, Artistic Director), The Joseph Papp Public Theater/ New York Shakespeare Festival (George C. Wolfe, Producer), the Relentless Theatre Company (Olivia Honegger, Artistic Director), Duke University, South Coast Repertory (David Emmes, Producing Artistic Director; Martin Benson, Artistic Director) and The Playwrights' Center (Polly Carl, Exectutive Director).

References to Salvador Dalí Make Me Hot received its world premiere at South Coast Repertory (David Emmes, Producing Artistic Director; Martin Benson, Artistic Director) in Costa Mesa, California, on January 28, 2000. Pacific Life Foundation was the Honorary Associate Producer. It was directed by Juliette Carrillo; scenic design was by Monica Raya, costume design was by Meg Neville, lighting design was by Geoff Korf, the composer and sound designer was Mitch Greenhill, the dramaturg was John Glore, the stage manager was Randall K. Lum and the production manager was Jeff Gifford. The cast was as follows:

MOON	Robert Montano
COYOTE	Victor Mack
CAT	Svetlana Efremova

GABRIELA	Ana Ortiz
MARTÍN	Wells Rosales
BENITO	Robert Montano

References to Salvador Dalí Make Me Hot received its New York premiere at The Joseph Papp Public Theater/New York Shakespeare Festival (George C. Wolfe, Producer; Fran Reiter, Executive Director; Rosemarie Tichler, Artistic Producer) on April 11, 2001. It was directed by Jo Bonney; scenic design was by Neil Patel, costume design was by Clint E. B. Ramos, lighting design was by David Weiner, sound design was by Donald DiNicola and Obadiah Eaves, original music was by Carlos Valdez, the dramaturg was John Dias and the production stage manager was Mike Schleifer. The cast was as follows:

MOON	Michael Lombard
COYOTE	Kevin Jackson
CAT	Kristine Nielsen
GABRIELA	Rosie Perez
MARTÍN	Carlo Alban
BENITO	John Ortiz

CHARACTERS

MOON, the moon in the sky, Gabriela's friend.
COYOTE, a wild one.
CAT, a fat one, Gabriela's pet.
MARTÍN, a Latino of fourteen, Gabriela's neighbor.
GABRIELA, a Latina, twenty-seven, an army housewife.
BENITO, a Latino, twenty-nine, Gabriela's husband,
a soldier.

SETTING

TIME: Shortly after the first Persian Gulf War.
PLACE: Barstow, California.

PROLOGUE
Gabriela's backyard. Night.

ACT ONE
Gabriela's backyard. Night.

ACT TWO
Gabriela's kitchen. 7:00 A.M.

ACT THREE
Gabriela's bedroom. Night.

ACT FOUR
Gabriela's backyard. 7:00 A.M.

And I'll sleep at your feet,
to watch over your dreams.

—FEDERICO GARCÍA LORCA
BLOOD WEDDING

Barstow, California. Night.

A cement-covered backyard. Cactus. Birds-of-paradise. Large spiny-edge aloe.

A wooden fence upstage. Beyond is the desert surrounded by low, barren mountains.

The Moon, standing on an old refrigerator, plays the violin: something lush and sentimental.

Lying on the ground, staring at the night sky, is Gabriela, a Latina of twenty-seven, wearing a T-shirt and tight cutoffs.

She talks to the Moon.

The Moon looks at her hungrily.

GABRIELA:

> *Before you're born, I wonder,*
> *as you looked around*
> *and took inventory of the womb . . .*
> *did it look like this?*
> *Did you see the moon and stars in there?*
> *Did you see floating bits of fire in there?*
> *Maybe you saw the food and air from your*
> *mother's bloodstream*

looking like constellations
against the deep, deep black
of your mother's night sky.
Like tonight.
¡Ay! I haven't had a lover's eyes
to look into for months.
I've been looking up
at the night sky instead . . .
watching the watchful moon.
Hey! What do you say, Moon?
What's the good word tonight?
I know you—yes, I do.
I've known you a long time.
I've felt your invisible fingers
tugging the liquids inside.
I've seen you eclipsed and moody.
And now you're so old, dear Moon,
you've outlived all your friends but me.
But that's okay because someday
we're going to shuffle off
to the grave—together—
wrinkled and slow:
two old companions
still in love,
still pinching each other's butts . . .

(Gabriela falls asleep as lights go down on her.)

ᔒ ACT ONE ᔒ

Lights up on the backyard. Gabriela is gone.
A female Cat and a male Coyote regard each other warily.
Coyote howls.

COYOTE:
    You don't trust me.

CAT:
    You're transparent.

COYOTE:
    You smell like soap.

CAT:
    You smell like shit.

COYOTE:
    Shit's natural. Remember natural?

CAT:
    You're full of secrets and worms.

COYOTE:

> You don't even know
> what fresh blood tastes like!

CAT:

> Hunted!

COYOTE:

> Brainwashed!

CAT:

> Unloved!

(Coyote howls with laughter.)

COYOTE:

> Unloved? I'm free!

CAT:

> Deluded.

COYOTE:

> And how do I keep my freedom?
> I don't worry about their love—
> their clinging, petting, hurtful . . .

CAT:

> Ay, jealous too!

COYOTE:

> Love with chains and flea collars attached.
> Love with no purpose to it,
> no reproduction, no passion.
> Love with violence implied.

12

CAT:

> *You have no idea how good it is.*

COYOTE:

> *You think everything that people do is good.*
> *Have you seen what they've done to my desert?*
> *The way the mountains*
> *are so nicely carved up—*
> *oh, such beautiful scars!—*
> *oh, the pretty bomb craters!—*
> *those sexy switchblade cuts*
> *in the flesh of the land!*
> *What kind of drugs*
> *do they put in your food?*

CAT:

> *How cold does it get at night, Coyote?*
> *How hard is that desert mattress you sleep on?*
> *What's it like to live*
> *in a world full of enemies?*

COYOTE:

> *Fun. Easy.*

CAT:

> *And the reason for the terror*
> *in your eyes? . . .*

COYOTE:

> *That's lethal energy you see in my eyes, Cat.*

CAT:

> *Ha! Scavenger energy.*
> *You let the real hunters*

do the killing:
let cars do the killing.
Then you come along,
tail between your legs,
sniffing around for the leftovers,
licking up the cold blood
and competing with the flies
for the juicy bits.

COYOTE:

Disinformation!

CAT:

Oh, such honor.
Nature at its best.
Majestic, awesome nature!

COYOTE:

You wouldn't survive a day—

CAT:

You're not even smart enough
to be a dog.
What exactly are you?
Half rat? Half mole?

COYOTE:

Not a single cold night!

CAT:

Poor me, with a home,
protection from the sun,
good eats, lots of toys:
Gabriela gives me everything.

COYOTE:

> *Toys and regular meals*
> *have made you fat.*
> *Blunted your instincts.*
> *Why don't you come out with me?*
> *Right now: do what I do for one night.*
> *No home, no petting,*
> *no place to hide.*
> *You couldn't do it, could you?*

CAT:

> *I don't have to prove a—*

COYOTE:

> *Prove it to yourself.*
> *Twenty-four hours in the wild.*
> *I'll take you to the desert.*
> *I'll take you hunting—*
> *lots of prey, natural enemies to dodge—*
> *you'll learn to look*
> *at your precious Gabriela*
> *from a real animal's point of view.*

CAT:

> *I take one step out of this yard,*
> *you and your little posse gang-attacks me.*

COYOTE:

> *You have my word.*

CAT *(Sizing him up)*:

> *Bet you'd love that . . . eating me.*
> *Tasting my round, warm meat.*
> *Domesticity has made my fatty parts*

soft, easy, and wet with juice.
I can see the saliva forming in your mouth
right now.

COYOTE:

That all you see?

CAT:

After you've swallowed my
moist outer layers—
you can chew my heart muscles
and give your jaws a real workout.
Take you all night to eat my thighs.

COYOTE:

Saliva's dripping down
and something else is coming up.

CAT:

Not really.

COYOTE:

Oh yeah.

CAT:

What a pig!

COYOTE:

You ain't never been laid
by a wild animal, have you?

CAT:

Is that what all this has been about?

COYOTE:

Like you didn't know!

CAT:

Barbarian!

COYOTE:

In the wild we really know how to love.
In the wild we do it under the savage sky,
get dirt in our eyes,
wet the ground with our funky juice.
You scream so hard your ancestors hear you.
It's not even sex, it's beyond sex,
beyond bodies, come on, Cat,
animal on animal.
I'll knock you around so hard
all nine of your lives will have orgasms.

CAT:

. . . All nine?

COYOTE:

Then you'll bear little coyote-cats—
tough mutant sons of bitches
who love the taste of blood
and the chase and the moonlit night.

CAT:

I can't do that—I'm fixed.

COYOTE:

Fixed? Fixed?
Oh, the beautiful English language!

CAT:

> Answer is No!

COYOTE:

> Aw, I wasn't going to beg!
> This is me begging!

> (Coyote begs for sex. He's shameless.)

CAT:

> Of course you're begging.
> You know what's in store for you.
> Nobody loves like a house cat.

COYOTE:

> What do I have to say?
> What do I have to promise?

CAT:

> Let me see.

COYOTE:

> A little lick? A sniff?
> Mind if I wet the edge
> of my tongue with your—?

CAT:

> What about some information?
> What happened to Pinkie Garcia?

COYOTE:

> Pinkie—who?

CAT:

> Persian. Light brown,
> long tail, weakness for grasshoppers.
> Missing two days, Coyote.

COYOTE:

> Don't know a thing about that . . .

CAT:

> What about Climber Rodriguez?
> Missing a week! Any clues?

COYOTE:

> You watch that tone of voice!

CAT:

> All the neighbor cats've been disappearing
> beginning with the first day
> of your arrival in Barstow.
> Making dirty war on my people!

> (Coyote grabs Cat.)

COYOTE (Laughing):

> You hate war, huh?
> War makes you comfortable, Cat.

> (Coyote kisses Cat.
> Cat is astonished by this.)

CAT:

> Those are very soft lips
> you have for a wild animal.

(Cat and Coyote howl in heat.
The backdoor opens.
Gabriela rushes out, holding a .9-millimeter revolver.)

GABRIELA:

    Enemies! Enemies!

COYOTE *(Terrified of humans)*:

    Holy God!

(Coyote hides.)

GABRIELA:

    Benito gave me this gun—
    and taught me how to use it!

CAT:

    It's just me, Gabriela!

GABRIELA:

    I defended our house in Germany.
    I can do it here.

CAT:

    Put the weapon down, nena.

GABRIELA:

    Who's out here with you?
    Freaks? Pukes?

COYOTE *(To Cat)*:

    Don't tell her about me, please—

GABRIELA:
> *Benito says freaks and pukes are buying*
> *up houses all over the country.*
> *He says they're well organized.*
> *They try to be your friend.*
> *They smile without fear of detection.*
> *But Benito trained me well:*
> *I'm on high alert.*
> *I won't let them sink their fangs*
> *into my unprotected psyche*
> *and drain the blood from my mind*
> *and turn me into* one of them.

CAT:
> *Really, Gabriela, you need to get laid.*

GABRIELA:
> Ay, *don't remind me!*

CAT:
> *When does Benito get back from the field?*—

GABRIELA:
> *I heard voices*—plural.

CAT *(A glance at Coyote)*:
> *Eh*—*no*—*it's just me*—*and the moon.*

GABRIELA:
> *The moon? The distant moon?*

COYOTE *(Sotto voce)*:
> *Bless you, gentle, sexy Cat!*

(A cactus moves.
Gabriela fires a shot at the cactus.)

MOON:

¡Una pistola! *What a woman!*

GABRIELA:

I've taken measurements.
When we first moved here
each of these cactus trees
was thirty feet away.
Then one night I heard curious sounds.
I walked out here and thought I saw
the cactus trees moving toward the house.
I ran inside and got a tape measure—
and sure enough! Twenty feet!
"Get over here, Benito," I shouted.
And Benito came and took measurements
and told me I was crazy
and went back to sleeping
and snoring and gyrating in the bed
and dreaming of Miss Panama
and Miss El Salvador
and Miss Teen Puerto Rico!
And I sit out here
and watch the cactus trees
inching closer and closer to my house
concealing dark spirits, hungry spirits,
secret-keepers and heartbreakers.
Yesterday I measured the trees.
Ten feet! Ten feet exactly!
What's it going to take to make
Benito believe me?
Why does he think I make it up?

MOON *(Frustrated)*:
> Ay, *when is she gonna get naked?*

GABRIELA:
> *Am I alone, Moon?*
> *Am I the only one?*
> *Does anyone in this desert,*
> *understand what I feel?*

MOON *(To Gabriela)*:
> *The people in this desert have their*
> *own problems,* nena.
> *In the house to your right*
> *an insomniac is looking through*
> *old photo albums.*
> *Her eyes trace memories back*
> *to their original moments:*
> *a fifteenth birthday party,*
> *a fight in a bar, a first kiss,*
> *a young boyfriend in uniform*
> *who wanted babies right away.*
> *She runs sleep-deprived fingers*
> *over black-and-white photos,*
> *trying to feel the skin*
> *of that old boyfriend.*
> *But the paper yields nothing.*
> *The moment before the photo was taken*
> *and the moment just after:*
> *these secret moments are exiled*
> *to those parts of the brain*
> *reserved for all the forgotten things.*
> *And this poor girl*
> *reenacts her nightly journey*
> *toward understanding her past—*

and every night,
inexplicably powerful currents
turn her away.

GABRIELA:
Poor girl.

MOON:
In the house to your left
an old man watches his old wife sleeping.
She breathes slowly
and he holds a mirror to her mouth.
A little cloud assures the old man
that she is alive.
He thinks of the day they first made love,
a sweet October day thousands of miles
and seasons from here.
He had never held a body
so rich with dreams
and she had never held a body
so hot and hungry,
and that first liquid night,
a night without food or sleep—
with my wicked light
coming in through their bedroom window—
as she lay in his exhausted arms . . .
he reached for a mirror
and put the mirror to her mouth
and she breathed on it—
proving to this young disbeliever
that she was indeed alive
and not a dream,
a woman and not a fabulous invention.
And now the old man is afraid

of life without her
and keeps a .9-millimeter in his house
and he checks his wife's dutiful breathing
and knows what to do in case it ever stops.

GABRIELA:
Poor old man.

CAT *(To the Moon)*:
Stop telling her those morbid stories
or she'll never rest!

GABRIELA:
Poor girl, poor old man:
poor people everywhere.

(Gabriela sobs.)

MOON:
¡Ay, pobrecita!
She needs me!

(The Moon puts down his violin and comes down from the sky.
The Moon has an immediate and powerful effect on Gabriela and Coyote.)

GABRIELA *(It feels good)*:
God!—it's like all my blood's
going crazy-insane in my body!
What the hell are you
doing to me, Moon?

MOON:
You need me!

(As the Moon gets closer to the ground, Coyote howls in pain.)

COYOTE:

> OH GOD, OH GOD—
> THE MOONLIGHT!
> IT HURTS MY BODY SO BAD!

(Cat goes to Coyote, who tries to run away as the Moon gets closer to the backyard.
> *Cat holds Coyote back.*
> *Gabriela watches the Moon approach, enthralled.)*

CAT:

> Coyote? Coyote?

COYOTE *(Struggling, in pain)*:
> Lunar light—
> sharp like daggers—
> cuts my skin—
> ricochets off my nerves—
> it's why coyotes howl
> at the full moon!

(Coyote runs off, howling.
> *Cat runs off after him.*
> *The Moon enters the backyard and goes to Gabriela.)*

GABRIELA:

> Ay, Moon, I feel so honored.

MOON *(To Gabriela)*:
> They say from the tears of women
> are civilizations made.

GABRIELA:
> *They really say that?*

MOON:
> *No, not really.*

GABRIELA:
> *Then why did you get my hopes up?*

MOON:
> *Shakespeare called me inconstant.*

GABRIELA:
> *I see why.*

MOON:
> *I never recovered from that.*
> *The bastard!*

GABRIELA *(Laughs)*:
> *Hey, Moon—*
> *Have you ever danced*
> *with a woman holding a gun?*

(Gabriela and the Moon dance.)

MOON:
> *From the tears of women*
> *come mathematics sonatas*
> *table manners the zipper*
> *the* merengue *editorial pages*
> *county fairs guitar strings*
> *lipstick and the fables*
> *of Jorge Luis Borges . . .*

GABRIELA:
> You're trying to get into
> my shorts, aren't you?

MOON (*Faster, more excited*):
> . . . brain surgery pickles
> Macondo Mecca
> the double play Bukowski tostones
> and Two Pieces of Bread
> Expressing the Sentiment of Love.

GABRIELA (*Gasps*):
> ¡Ay! *References to Salvador Dalí*
> *make me hot!*

(Gabriela kisses the Moon passionately.)

GABRIELA (*To Moon*):
> *Those are very soft lips*
> *you have for a celestial object.*

(Martín, a fourteen-year old Latino boy, appears at the fence. He looks at the yard through a telescope.
> *As he continues to dance with Gabriela, the Moon notices Martín and snickers.)*

MOON:
> *Aw, look at the little perv—*
> *back for more . . .*

MARTÍN:
> *Gabriela's my religion, Moon.*
> *My altered state of grace.*

MOON *(To Martín)*:
> *Give it up, little boy,*
> *she's outta your league.*

MARTÍN:
> *I look at her ass and I hallucinate.*
> *I'm all falling into her like I'm dying*
> *and her body is the grave*
> *and I got buried between her loins*
> *and get to spend eternity*
> *swimming in her*
> *like a warm, creamy, gooey bath!*

MOON:
> *You want me to kick your ass?!*

MARTÍN *(To audience)*:
> *I've been coming every night*
> *for two months*
> *to watch Gabriela walk across*
> *the yard, back and forth,*
> *like totally naked—*
> *hoping like a sad son of a bitch*
> *to see her thing!*
> *But it's weird—tonight*
> *a strange transformation's*
> *taking place in me as I watch her*
> *dance with the pushy moon.*
> *I'm bathed in his weird, magnetic light*
> *and I'm changed completely!*
> *The little boy who wanted*
> *a cheap, dick-centered thrill is dead.*
> *In his place, out of his cold remains,*
> *rises a young man full of mature,*

*virile desire: a young man
unafraid to take on all rivals:
a young man in love with love!*

*(Martín jumps down into the yard.
Gabriela talks to the Moon. She and Martín speak in
sync.)*

GABRIELA/MARTÍN:

*I (wanted/want) to touch (Benito's/her) skin
because I (wanted/want) to learn something.
Not about the temperature of (his/her) body.
Or how soft the hairs on (his/her) thing are.
Touching (his/her) skin (had/has) to do with . . .
testing the vibrations . . .
down past the glands and mute corpuscles . . .
down where bones talk
and the human body hums with music . . .
I (wanted/want) to find out
if we're tuned the same way.
What's the pitch of (his/her) soul?
Can I hear it if I tried?
Will I ever be able to sing along with it?*

MARTÍN *(To the Moon)*:

I think she wants my ass.

GABRIELA:

*But the idea of exploring
the notes and chords of each other's souls—
feels impossible now . . .*

MARTÍN:

*A-ha!
She and the husband are incompatible!*

MOON *(To Gabriela)*:
> *Yes, actually, I do, actually,*
> *I, yes actually, yes, I do actually*
> *want to get into your shorts.*

MARTÍN *(To the Moon)*:
> *Get in line you big stupid rock!*

GABRIELA:
> *The dreams of my husband are a mystery to me.*
> *What secrets have abducted Benito from me?*
> *Was it the war?*

MOON *(To Martín)*:
> *I'll kick your ass, punk!*

GABRIELA:
> *What's funny is people always say,*
> *if you want mystery, go to the moon.*

MARTÍN:
> *He ain't mysterious.*
> *He's been explored too much.*
> *Too many little nasty footprints*
> *and American flags on him!*

MOON:
> *I'll knock your block off—*

GABRIELA:
> *I say the deepest secrets*
> *and the most confusing mysteries*
> *aren't on the moon,*
> *they're in the heart of the person*
> *who lies next to you in bed every night.*

MARTÍN:
I'll let you in,
mi vida, mi luz, mi alma!

(Martín pushes the Moon away from Gabriela.)

GABRIELA:
Martín!

MARTÍN:
Martín del Cuerpo Grande y Peludo,
at your service.
And the moon can't love you like I can,
mi cielo, mi corazon, mi sangre!

GABRIELA:
What are you again? Twelve?

MARTÍN:
Fourteen, mi amor.
And growing.
I have new hair
about to happen all over my body.

GABRIELA:
Remember my husband?
Seven-foot-six?
Two-eighty-five?
Owner of this and other firearms?

MOON *(To Martín):*
What do you mean I can't love her
like you can?

MARTÍN *(To the Moon)*:
> You're incontinent.
> Shakespeare said.

MOON:

> "Inconstant" not "incontinent,"
> you little fart!

(The Moon and Martín fight.
> *The Moon takes the gun from Gabriela and pistol-whips*
Martín. Martín falls hard.)

GABRIELA *(To the Moon)*:
> Look what you did!
> You're supposed to be romantic.

MOON:

> I did it for you.
> How romantic can you get, mujer?

GABRIELA *(To Martín)*:
> Kid. Hey kid.

MOON *(To Gabriela)*:
> Does this mean it's over?—

GABRIELA *(To the Moon)*:
> Just get out of my face, all right?

(Gabriela tries to revive Martín.
> *The dejected Moon goes back into the sky.)*

MOON:

> I shouldn't get involved with people.
> I should just watch.

That's what the moon does best.
Watches and bears witness—
then silently reports to you
through your dreams.
What are premonitions, hunches, déjà vu,
and the little voice in your head?
That's me—
whispering nightly in your ear,
hoping to give you a fighting chance
in this hard, carnivorous world.
Yes, Gabby, the trees are closing in on you.
Your visions of dark and hungry spirits are true.
And your husband's mind and heart
seem to've been sucked out of him.
So listen to the shadows, nena.
Pay attention to the lines between the lines.
That's the only way you're going
to survive out here,
at the edge of nowhere.

(The Moon is back in the sky.
Gabriela holds Martín.)

MARTÍN *(Semi-conscious)*:
. . . when they bury virgins they say
that the grass never grows on the grave . . .

GABRIELA:
People say a lot of bullshit.
For you love is a mystery and a poem.
For me it's bad habits and
bones and hair and musky smells
and tricks that don't work anymore.

MARTÍN *(Semi-conscious)*:
>   *. . . I'm gonna die an old man*
>   *who ain't never touched a woman's thing . . .*

GABRIELA:
>   *I don't know what I'm going to do*
>   *when he comes home in the morning.*
>   *The house will seem too small.*
>   *He'll cry and shout in his sleep*
>   *as the truth fights to get out*
>   *while he dreams.*

MARTÍN *(Semi-conscious)*:
>   *Sleep with me.*

GABRIELA:
>   *The person I've chosen*
>   *left his body at the house*
>   *while his mind and soul travel*
>   *the solar system looking for love and laughs.*
>   *I wonder if I can get him back.*
>   *I wonder if I want him back.*
>   *I wonder if I care anymore.*
>   *I wonder if he cares where I've been.*

MARTÍN *(Semi-conscious)*:
>   *I know you want babies.*

GABRIELA *(A sad laugh)*:
>   *I'll sleep with you.*
>   *But this is not*
>   *what you had in mind.*

(Gabriela lies on the ground next to Martín. They're not touching.)

MARTÍN *(Semi-conscious)*:
    Finally.
    In the arms of a woman.
    It's better than I ever imagined.

GABRIELA:
    Tomorrow morning is going to bring changes.
    Big, great, awful changes.
    I'm ready, Martín, are you?
    I'm ready to make it happen—
    and I'm ready for whatever happens to me.
    Let it come.
    Let the awful and beautiful changes come.

(Gabriela and Martín fall asleep side by side.
    The Moon plays the violin: something sad, as the lights fade to black.)

⚞ ACT TWO ⚟

Seven A.M. Lights up on Gabriela's kitchen. Refrigerator, sink, stove, kitchen table and chairs.

Benito, Gabriela's husband, a Latino sergeant of twenty-nine, in full desert camouflage uniform, including web gear, stands surrounded by duffel bags.

Gabriela wears a short skirt, tank top and no shoes.

She and Benito haven't seen each other in two months.

BENITO: Where were you?
GABRIELA: Backyard.
BENITO: What's in the backyard?
GABRIELA: Slept there.
BENITO: Bed on fire?
GABRIELA: Just did, that's all.

(They kiss briefly.)

BENITO: Huh. What's the coffee situation?
GABRIELA: As you wish, master.
BENITO: Call me master a lot, I really like it.

(Gabriela makes coffee.)

GABRIELA: Lost a shitload of weight, soldier.
BENITO: God bless them MREs.
GABRIELA: And nice circles under the eyes.
BENITO: Ain't slept in forty-eight.
GABRIELA: When are them fuckers gonna stop abusing my pretty, old man, huh?
BENITO: New deodorant? You smell weird . . .
GABRIELA: At least I don't smell like tank fuel.
BENITO *(Looking at her hair)*: You didn't mention the thing, the 'do, the nest . . .
GABRIELA: I was bored. You hate it.
BENITO: *Ages* you—but just a little—hardly nothing!—five or six years, max!
GABRIELA *(Can't help laughing)*: Here's your stupid gun.

(Gabriela hands Benito his .9-millimeter.)

BENITO: Not gun, *weapon*. Your gun hangs between your legs.
GABRIELA: Nothing hangs between my legs, sergeant.

(Benito eyes her up and down with great male appreciation.)

BENITO: 'Cept me. Gabby. Oh, squeezable, eatable, good to the last drop . . .
GABRIELA: Before you get all worked up, I got a question. It's gonna sound, like, stupid, but fucking laugh, I'll kick your ass back to Fort Irwin. Did you see the moon last night?
BENITO *(Still on Gabby's body)*: . . . better'n pogey bait . . .
GABRIELA: Did you see the moon last night? I really gotta know this, Benito . . .

(Gabriela looks at him like his answer will decide every-thing.)

BENITO: The moon? Why on earth is a working man looking at the moon for?

GABRIELA *(Disappointed)*: 'Cause it was fucking huge, 'cause you used to . . .

BENITO: The moon wearing a dress? Jerking itself off?

(Gabriela ignores him and opens the refrigerator.)

GABRIELA: We're outta milk.

BENITO *(Thinking about it)*: Like maybe that's why they call it the Milky Way. The moon whacks off and comes all over the sky and *that's* how the Milky Way was born.

GABRIELA: Matter-of-fact, wiseass, that ain't how it happened—

BENITO: No, no, please, not a lecture on . . .

GABRIELA: Fact is, the Milky Way was born outta, you know, little fluctuation thingies in space-time at the moment of the Big Bang.

BENITO: I like the way you say, "Big Bang."

GABRIELA *(Starting to leave)*: I'm going out, pick up some milk.

BENITO: *Now?*

GABRIELA: Cigarettes too, master?

BENITO: Stop calling me master, wench!

GABRIELA: Well, if you don't wanna come into the milk container and pour *that* in your cof—

BENITO: What is your God-given problem? And how come there's no milk?

GABRIELA: Christ, I'm going . . .

BENITO: What're you doing all day? It's the first. I'm back today. It's been today since like forever.

GABRIELA: I use milk. It runs out. I didn't go shopping. Why? I don't know.

BENITO: Too busy with the lesbian hair?—

GABRIELA: Too busy boning that cute Mexican boy lives next—

BENITO: *Coño*, girl, you are like . . . I don't know what . . .

GABRIELA: Yeah, well, welcome home.

BENITO: Feel welcomed too. It's been forever since I got kissed serious or groped around here—and the first thing you want is, you see my face, you're out the door!

(Benito goes to the refrigerator and opens it.)

An empty fridge! That's like apocalyptic even! Ice cube trays full of sand. Not even a beer.

GABRIELA: Don't check the cabinets.

(Benito checks the cabinets. They're full of:)

BENITO: Catfood. Catfood. Catfood. What? You mad at me or something? Mad at little old Benito for something he ain't got clue one what he done?

GABRIELA: Not exactly mad and learn *English*, please.

BENITO: "Not exactly mad"? Now that strikes terror. *Oye.* We're starting over. Restarting the clock back.

(Benito exits the kitchen and reenters.)

BENITO: Hi, honey, I'm home! Back from the field. From two hundred cancer-making degrees. From boredom so perfect and rare it lacks a name. From nothing good to look at but the backsides of doorknobs with their thumb up their ass. Farm boys so interbred they can't tell a M-16 from the gun between their legs.

GABRIELA *(Can't help laughing)*: Why are soldiers such children?

BENITO: Better haul that face over here, *coño*!

(Benito grabs Gabriela and kisses her. This kiss evolves rapidly and they're all over each other.
    Benito tries to unzip her skirt and take off his clothes during the following.)

GABRIELA: For a guy who ain't slept in forty-eight hours—

BENITO *(Taking off his shirt)*: Missed you like a sad broken son of a bitch.

GABRIELA *(Kissing him)*: You taste so good, damn you, *Negro* . . . and I'm sorry I'm the dragon lady from hell, but I got—*Benito*—when I'm sleeping, I get these—what are you doing?

BENITO *(Stripping fast)*: Thought since you ain't seen a man in two months, you'd like to see what a man looks like.

GABRIELA: I think I'm getting my period.

BENITO: Hey, I'm liberal. Anyway, you think I'm afraid of a little blood?

GABRIELA: Like living with the author of the Song of Songs, I swear.

BENITO *(Working her zipper)*: You call Costco . . . ?

GABRIELA: Just give me a minute to catch my breath . . .

BENITO *(Working her zipper)*: . . . tell 'em you're out sick today? . . .

GABRIELA: Maybe let's get to know each other first?

BENITO *(Working her zipper)*: Why?

GABRIELA: Pull that zipper any lower and I'm yelling rape.

BENITO *(Thinks it's a joke)*: You're so funny.

GABRIELA: Benito I'm fuckin' not *fucking* with you!

(Gabriela pulls away, pulling up her zipper, shaking, fighting for control.
Benito looks at her for a cold, long moment.)

BENITO: I walked into some other dude's nightmare, *hija*, 'cause you ain't you.

(Benito collects his gear and starts to leave.)

GABRIELA: You know the cat's missing?

(Benito stops, turns to her.)

BENITO: When I'm home from the field we leave words and other debris at the door, then close the motherfucking door.

GABRIELA: Did you hear what I said about the cat?

BENITO: Ain't the pussy I'm interested in right now . . .

GABRIELA: *Ay, Dios,* man, God, shit: go play with yourself!

BENITO: Is it my fault you got the Ass of Heaven?

GABRIELA: How many ways I gotta tell you I'm not some strip-artist whore-bitch you picked up in some German night club?—

BENITO: Then don't wear that skirt!

GABRIELA: Clawing at me like I'm a piece of twenty-five-dollar street trash—

BENITO: You know where I can get it for twenty-five? Damn, point the way, girl!

GABRIELA: And it's hot. I wear this 'cause we live in Barstow and it's *July?*

BENITO: Okay, *nena,* that was a joke, I will not claw you, I will respect you, 'cause you are the farthest thing on earth from a twenty-five-dollar-German-whore-bitch-street-bitch-German-thing, really, I tell you the God's honest.

GABRIELA: You know you get crazy-insane when you're impatient?

BENITO: I'm human and male—so fuck me.

GABRIELA: You wanna hear about the cat or not?

BENITO: Bet half the company's in bed with their old ladies.

GABRIELA: Their old ladies are sex slaves and I'm not.

BENITO: *My* bad luck!

(Gabriela cleans obsessively: washing dishes, wiping down countertops, etc.)

GABRIELA: I got home last night in a great mood. Had a great class. The kind that makes your mind go fucking ballistic. You wanna know why?

BENITO: No, no, please don't tell me about your . . .

GABRIELA: We watch the night sky, what do we see? Billions of galaxies right? But *now* we think all those galaxies don't really exist . . .

BENITO: We do?

GABRIELA: 'Cause in space, light gets twisted . . . 'cause gravity bends it all up . . . so looking at space is like looking through thousands of mirrors reflecting the same handful of galaxies over and over and over and over. That fucking wild or what? The universe is an *optical illusion*. And it's lonelier than we ever thought.

BENITO: This kitchen's proof of that . . .

GABRIELA: So anyway, I got home from school, I call her, nothing. Then all night I'm hearing coyotes setting up camp under my window, whole posses, like, I don't know, like, like . . .

BENITO: How come with you everything's gotta be like something else? Why can't shit just be what it is with you?

GABRIELA *(Ignoring him)*: . . . like they opened up an asylum full of coyotes and they all parked their crazy asses in my backyard—howling like they're getting stabbed by the moonlight.

BENITO: Oh, that's clear, thank you.

GABRIELA: I think they ate my cat. One you gave me for my birthday?

BENITO: Maybe I'll get that milk—

GABRIELA: The cat's devoured. Mind's all like—Christ *no!*—thinking of her maimed to death by wild animals chewing her flesh. And I think it's gotta mean something, Benito. Like the Buddha says: there's no coincidences.

BENITO: The Buddha?

GABRIELA: I decided that life is fulla signals that teach you shit. And I've been blind like I didn't wanna know. So I'm thinking that something like this doesn't happen for no reason, the cat, and I'm pondering: what other signs of important things have I been missing lately? You know. About us. And shit that's going on.

BENITO (*Making a shopping list*): Beer, milk, bullshit remover, strap-ons—oops, scratch the—

GABRIELA: Benito—for crying—sometimes I think you work overtime not to hear me! Unlike you, for months I got no one to share shit with—and now, without the cat, it's even lonelier here . . .

BENITO: Loneliness is your choice, *nena*.

GABRIELA: No one sane chooses this.

BENITO: If you didn't look down on all my buds and their wives who tried hard to make friends with you and found it *impossible*.

GABRIELA: Those Barbie dolls your buddies are saddled with? Those wooden pieces of perpetual blow-job machines?

BENITO: This language is offensive. Period.

GABRIELA: I tried making friends. But it's a scientific fact: the brain can only gossip 'bout soap operas for so long before it starts to puke on itself. Or else we're in prayer meetings trashing queers and blacks or we're sitting around with cucumbers in our mouths, practicing blow jobs.

BENITO: You were getting a valuable lesson!

GABRIELA: *¡Coño!* Everything's a joke to you! You don't *listen*! Meanwhile, I'm the one stuck in the desert and it's like, like . . .

BENITO: Wait, I'll do it. It's like . . . a nuclear beast ate up the whole world with all its flaming teeth, and left nothing but the deep-fried leftovers in the Tupperware of Human Shit.

GABRIELA: Not even close. You don't see it like a civilian does. Like I do—all fulla scars and bomb craters. Fucking ugly cactus closing in on you. I'm a tropical woman, Benny, I'm not used to this.

BENITO: Grand Concourse ain't tropical.

GABRIELA: This stupid desert *fools* you. You think it's safe. Think you can lie on the ground and stare at the moon.

BENITO: *Ay,* this moon crap again. All the moon is is future landfill, Gab.

GABRIELA: Shakespeare didn't think so. He called it inconstant.

BENITO: And I care!

GABRIELA: Stupid you: you go out in the desert and coyotes jump your ass and eat you. The sun bakes you. The night-cold freezes blood. The bigness of it scares your heart and makes it stop. Okay—so then you *don't* go outside. You're stuck *inside*—over at the friggin' Costco or the commissary on post or a sorry-ass movie in Victorville with the Barbie dolls. But strangers in the dark air-conditioning make you feel small and stupid. Couples with their fancy fingers all inside each other's pants remind you your old man's not around. On the movie screen is life all full of big blood and sex and people making perfect funny jokes every time. Like to remind you nobody really laughs in your world when you're alone. And that's what my life has been like, Benito, okay? And you know what? It really sucks! It's really a shitty thing to do to a person!

BENITO: So what are you telling me? Tell me what you're telling me and stop telling me the other shit you're not telling me.

GABRIELA: They stick you in a war. I don't see you for a year. I finally get you home *minutes,* it feels like, not enough time to take your temperature, get used to your smell or know why you cry in your sleep—boom!—we're shipped to the desert and you're off to the field again!

BENITO: This is my job we're talking about, right? What are you saying about my job?

GABRIELA: I'm saying fuck your job, okay?

BENITO: That's telling me something. I'm telling you—not to worry about the desert, in a year it's Germany.

GABRIELA: Oh, *that's* a step up. That's the highway to self-respect.

BENITO: Well, what am I supposed to do?! Will you tell me that?! Dammit to fucking hell on *earth*, Gabriela!

GABRIELA: Don't yell at—

BENITO: I am in the—what? Let's read aloud the little tag here on my . . . sez—ARMY! I am in the army. In the army you travel. That's what the army is, homegirl! A great motherfucker of a travel agency. And they don't recommend all nice and sweat-free: *they order you!* One year it's Germany where the whole country is full of Germans, and I'm sorry but we tried to get rid of the Germans, but dammit, the Germans didn't want to go! Then the next year it's the desert. Oh, the desert's hot! It's boring! Full o' vermin! The army wives never finished preschool. I hate the blow-job lessons! But in case you didn't notice, your car runs on oil and there's this place where oil comes from and everybody wants a piece of that sucker but if you want anything on God's goofy earth you gotta display the size of your *cojones*, and oh my God, the Middle East is in a desert!

GABRIELA: I know where the damn—

BENITO *(On a roll)*: We train soldiers in the art of desert warfare—where?—in the desert! *¡Ay Dios mio!* I go out to the field for months at a time—why?—'cause they pay my ass! I don't like it. I don't want it. But I didn't feel like cutting pineapple the rest of my life in some Puerto Rican Plantation of Death. I told you I'm staying in the army twenty years and retiring at the ripe old age of thirty-eight, pocket a full pension and never for a second sweat the money shit for as long as I have life, as long as *we* have life, never. Told you that our first date, running out of that bar with skinheads chasing us. I got nine years left on the meter, Gabby. More than half the way there. So the next nine years, *nena*, is Germany or the desert, Germany or the desert, snow or sand, Nazis or knuckleheads, back and forth like that assuming war don't break out and I'm not protecting goatherders in Somalia! That's the trip you signed on to take. Are there any questions, private?

GABRIELA: No sir, master, sir.

(Gabriela pours all the coffee she made down the sink.)

BENITO: You gotta stop acting like you know more than everybody. Like the Buddha says: it's a turn off.

GABRIELA: Oh, *fuck it*—now we're just talking in and out of the same three sentences—as if, like, more words means more communicating. Ain't that a joke? I'm going for that milk.

(Gabriela goes for her car keys.)

BENITO: You think you're the only one. You got no clue of my life's insanity out there—'cause I make this army shit look easy. Look graceful. That's why you don't know jack how fucked it is for me.

GABRIELA: Christ, the man can't stop yapping . . .

BENITO: The last month in the field, for me, I got my ass stuck in Star Wars, Gabby, okay? That's where I was. *Inside.* Behind a *desk.* In front of a *computer screen* watching the grunts and gun bunnies go through their mock battles and combat simulations. I went outta my mind. I'm going to the captain, going, sir, if I'm gonna play GI Joe I wanna be in an M1A1 or jumping out of a chopper or blowing expensive stuff up, not in a goddamn *building* with *air-*

conditioning. But no. Captain rules. So I'm doing Star Wars now.

GABRIELA: That's cause for bitching? You're sitting in air-conditioning! It's the middle of the Mojave!

BENITO: Gabriela, I don't wanna sit. Sitting is for *officers*. For *points*. A man does not sit when he *works*.

GABRIELA: Yeah, but, think—you could—maybe there's training here you can pick up, you know, learn a, you know . . .

BENITO: Skill? That I can use in the "real world"?

GABRIELA: It saves on your body, you don't gotta wreck yourself . . .

BENITO: Just waste away like some puke college professor—

GABRIELA: I just think you could be better than some common foot soldier—

BENITO: I am no common anything, okay?

GABRIELA: But maybe the captain—

BENITO: What? Wants to get his prep school lips around my joint? He pulled me out of a line of men. This has nothing to do with me at all.

GABRIELA: So what are you afraid of?

BENITO: Go shoot yourself.

GABRIELA: No, I'm asking you something—

BENITO: No, no, no, no. I know how the mind is working now, it's so obvious, Gabby, c'mon: "Benito hates to use his brain. Benito don't know a good thing when it's staring straight into his baboon face!" You know what I turned into out there? A man watching other men work. Then I had to write a "narrative description" of all the things the men did while they worked. So I'm in front of a half-billion dollars of pure high-tech and with two little chopstick fingers I take a half-hour to type out three sentences and I can't spell half the words I have to write. That's my job.

GABRIELA: But nobody shot at you, did they?

(Benito throws his arms in the air and sits at a kitchen chair, his back to Gabriela.)

BENITO: What did I do? What did I do? Huh? I just want you to take your top off!

GABRIELA *(Sarcastic)*: Stop, you're getting me so horny.

BENITO: Damn, I'm, like, out there, in no-man's-land, pretending to have war except all the hardware is more real than me, but the conflict is a game, it's fiction, and that's my job, and I come home to you, all beautiful, like what you see after death and the angels greet you in the morning, and you hope, you know, God allows sex with the angels in Heaven maybe once in a while if you're extra good around Christmas, but everything between us is real war, honey, and it's getting old real fast, baby, I'm telling you.

(Benito closes his eyes.)

GABRIELA: Tell you what *I* don't get, *Negro.* How, like, a feeling, which is made of nothing, can burn a hole in your stomach . . . or make a lump in your throat heavy as a man. A lump you wake up with . . . and stays with you until you go to bed . . .

BENITO *(Eyes closed)*: Enough. I just got back from the field. You don't know me. I don't know you. It's your usual freak-out when I come home.

GABRIELA: But it's the first time you were in the field since the war and I'm like all outta practice being your wife . . .

BENITO *(Eyes still closed, sleepy)*: . . . we'll get over it, like we always . . .

GABRIELA: . . . and I'm having dreams every single night and all of them want me to test you . . .

BENITO *(About to fall asleep)*: Stop. Just stop with that. Don't tell me no more about dreams . . .

(Silence. Benito falls asleep in the chair. Gabriela takes off his boots.)

GABRIELA: Jesus, I forget how much space you take up. Soon you'll be leaving pubes on the tile. And, like, if I think things now—am I gonna know which thoughts are mine 'cause they're mine, or they're mine 'cause you put them there . . .

(Martín enters holding a large cardboard box.)

MARTÍN: Where's my reward, woman?

(Gabriela sees her cat inside the box.)

GABRIELA *(To Cat)*: I was ready to call the fucking morgues for you!

MARTÍN: Found her surrounded by coyotes all salivating and doing the humpy motion with their torsos. She was next to a cat skeleton. We think it's the remains of Pinky Garcia.

GABRIELA *(To Cat)*: Better not catch no rabies, you!

MARTÍN: Looks like she got some animal-on-animal last night.

GABRIELA *(To Cat)*: Good thing you're fixed. I don't feel like raising a bunch of mutant coyote-cats.

MARTÍN *(Motioning toward Benito)*: No one's worried about the noise level?

GABRIELA: He'll sleep for seven straight, I swear, *days.*

(Gabriela puts the Cat in another room.)

MARTÍN: I'm going to the store, you want anything?

(Gabriela gives Martín money.)

GABRIELA: Ten for the cat rescue. Now go.

MARTÍN: You saying you don't want me around no more?

GABRIELA: I'm saying my old man's back from the field and has a limited ser.se of humor when it comes to who he thinks wants to fuck me.

MARTÍN: Wow, that sounds so sexual.

GABRIELA: How do you even know concepts of the human body?

MARTÍN: I'm only saying I know you want babies. I'm old enough to get you pregnant.

GABRIELA: In your fantasy world.

MARTÍN: In biology world, *mujer*.

GABRIELA: Just hope your dick's not a small as your brain!

MARTÍN: That's so mean!

GABRIELA: Look, fine, we had some fun, playing touch football, whatever. But recess time is over, the bell rang, junior, time to get on the school bus and go home.

MARTÍN: I'm growing pecs.

GABRIELA: My man is back and he's got rules and regulations.

MARTÍN: I wouldn't ask you to serve me. I can wash my own *ropa*. I would bring you hot *huevos* in the morning. Read the *periodico* to you. Put your *pelo* up in bobby pins. Keep your *piso* waxed. Your *cocina* full of canned creamy soup and Cocoa Puffs. Okay, *nena*?

GABRIELA: Out, please.

MARTÍN: I don't need to be big and strong. I can handle your nightmares if you tell them to me. I love a house full of singing and fresh desert air. I'll even tolerate your cat. Don't answer right away, Gabby. But think about it.

GABRIELA: You're fourteen.

MARTÍN: Can I see it?

GABRIELA: No.

(She pushes him out the door.)

MARTÍN: I saw you sleeping in the backyard again. I know this isn't paradise, Gabby. Hey—wasn't that a great fucking moon last night?

(Martín gives Gabriela a kiss on the cheek and goes.
Gabriela looks at Benito for a long moment, watching him sleep. She sits cross-legged on the floor, facing him. She takes off her top, exposing herself to Benito, who continues to sleep.)

BENITO *(In his sleep)*: Gabby's having dreams . . .

GABRIELA: . . . her dreams are full of broken moonlight, Benito . . . her dreams are full of moist sex and the dirty smell of sweat . . . her dreams level civilizations and make them grateful for chaos and heavy breathing and whirl-winds . . .

BENITO: . . . Gabby's having awful dreams . . .

(Gabriela holds herself, trying hard to keep from crying, as Benito sleeps. The lights fade to black.)

⚔ ACT THREE ⚔

That night.

Lights up on Gabriela's bedroom. On the walls: photos of tanks, Benito's military citations, a poster of Salvador Dalí's Two Pieces of Bread Expressing the Sentiment of Love, *and a black velvet unicorn poster. Military swords are displayed over the headboard. A stack of books and a telescope sit on a table next to the bed.*

The light of the Moon comes in through the windows.

Outside there are occasional maddening howls of coyotes.

Benito lies in bed, fast asleep, bootless and minus the web gear, but otherwise dressed as he was at the end of Act Two.

Gabriela lies at his side, dressed in sweatshirt and sweatpants. She holds a mirror to Benito's mouth, watching his breath cloud the glass, leaning close to him.

Benito cries in his sleep. He sounds like a wounded coyote. He thrashes. Alarmed, Gabriela shakes Benito awake.

He wakes with a gasp, and without looking or thinking takes a swing at Gabriela. She instinctively pulls back and Benito misses. He's disoriented, breathing hard.

BENITO: *Never . . .* never wake me up like that, *nena,* if you don't want your teeth on the floor.

GABRIELA (*Shaken*): I'm sorry. I forgot. It's been a while, remember?

BENITO: Shit. Shit. That whacked my nerves up pretty bad. It's the same day?

GABRIELA: I'm not sure what's the day.

BENITO: You okay? I didn't—?

GABRIELA: Some instinct in me remembered you've been doing that since the war.

BENITO: Everything's swirling in this room, *carajo*. Must be all the drugs I don't take but wish I did . . .

(*Groaning, Benito unsteadily gets out of bed and goes to the bathroom. Gabriela talks to Benito as he takes a leak.*)

GABRIELA: You were talking in your dreams.

BENITO (*Offstage*): I never dream.

GABRIELA: Everyone does. It's only human.

BENITO (*Off*): I ain't only human. I'm human-plus.

GABRIELA: I heard you making noises. Like something was coming outta someplace in you, someplace down and low, like where your bones talk.

BENITO (*Off*): This just in: bones don't talk.

GABRIELA: If they did. You cry in your sleep too. So quiet maybe only a bat could hear it. So secret, too, the air that brings it up from inside you hardly makes a scratch in the mirror I held all day long to your mouth, 'cause I was afraid you were dead sometimes.

BENITO (*Off*): I'm so glad to know that.

GABRIELA (*More to herself*): It's kinda screwed up: of all the parts of the body, only the brain gets the power to speak. I'd love to know what your stomach thinks.

(*Benito comes in from the bathroom.*)

BENITO: My stomach thinks you're mental. Other organs have their own viewpoints on this.

(During the following, Benito strips down to his boxers—a not-so-subtle striptease for Gabriela.)

GABRIELA *(Amused):* . . . Okay, here's what I don't get. How come in eleven years in the army I never heard you or any of your pinhead friends say one honest patriotic thing?

BENITO *(Stripping):* I love my country. It's the people in it I hate.

GABRIELA: Makes me laugh to think of you risking your life for a bunch of tree huggers.

BENITO *(Stripping):* Immigrants, welfare queens . . .

GABRIELA: Welfare? C'mon! What was the house in Germany we didn't pay for? That pumped-up car? That ain't tax-payer money being wasted?

BENITO: Taxpayer's getting a lean, mean fighting machine—with a nice ass.

GABRIELA: Who can't stop crying in his sleep like an infant baby.

(Benito gets into bed.)

BENITO: Every soldier does that. It's nothing. Justifies the combat pay.

GABRIELA: If it's nothing what's the big crime in telling me?

BENITO: . . . And how come there's sand in here? And what's with the ugly pajamas?

GABRIELA: You think, oh, your mind's this distant private place, what happens in there only happens to you—but it happens to me, too—

BENITO: It's gotta lighten up in here or I'll mistake this bed for the bottom of Death Valley.

GABRIELA: I tell you every passing thing that hits my mind, Benito.

BENITO *(Sarcastic)*: And it ain't as boring as scrubbing a barracks' floor with a Q-tip.

(Gabriela looks at Benito. A silent moment.)

GABRIELA: Oh. Boring, huh? Not exciting enough, huh?

(Gabriela gets out of bed and changes her clothes.)

BENITO: What are you doing?

GABRIELA: If I hurry, I can catch the second half of my class.

BENITO: Tonight? You're going to school—?

GABRIELA: It's been tonight since about forever.

BENITO: You always quit your classes when I'm home from the field. That's been the deal—

GABRIELA: But in this one, we spend hours looking up—and I never do that in real life, look up. It makes me aware of the fucking universe, okay?

BENITO: Gabby, for crying out loud—

GABRIELA: *Exactly* what you been doing all day in your sleep. Driving me crazy with the sound of pain busting your gut. Making me wonder what's in there, thinking the worst, holding my breath for an answer, getting *zero*. You want me to stay? Give me a husband that's more than a body in my bed, okay?

BENITO: Maybe *you* get something outta pulling barbed wire out of a person, but I'm the one who suffers doing that. Humans like to put pain to *rest*.

GABRIELA: Silence never rests nothing.

BENITO: *Oyeme, nena, por Dios*, it was . . . nothing. A thing. I did a thing, after the ground war I never told you about. Messed my head a little. Okay? Now get back in—

GABRIELA (*Getting her telescope*): School's an hour away, I'll be back in—

BENITO: The *balls* you have! Dang!

GABRIELA: Dang? You expect me to lie in bed and spread my legs—for who? A stranger? Benito—hello—who are you?

BENITO: One tired son of a bitch is who.

GABRIELA: I promised to God that whatever they throw at you, I'd help you take care of it, if you let me, if I know how. I look at you, I see like shrapnel I gotta pull outta you and dead soldiers to bury. But I can't do it if I don't know what happened.

BENITO: You're not gonna like it, Gab.

GABRIELA: I'm not promising to like it, I'm not promising not to be mad, I'm promising to listen.

(*Beat.*)

BENITO: Okay, the war was over. We were pacifying little towns. So small you're afraid the wind will blow them away. So the ragheads had big-time curfews—like if three or more hang out on a street corner, boom, automatic arrest, no questions asked, off to Saudi and them in their monkey-language all pissed off at you. So the scene's all pacified and I'm just hangin' with a couple of tread-heads contemplating playing spades on the downtime—it's *that* mellow—when some idiot fires a rocket at the APC I'm standing next to and blows a hole in it the size of Kuwait and decimates one of my corporals. And I'm telling you, I'm tripping. I'm like insane over this event. I'm stomping around the desert like baby Godzilla, cursing the little Persian freaks and I got wild, Gabby, you know what I did? The war is over and you know what I did? I called for fire. I'm the F.O. out there and I get on the horn and I call an air strike and I leveled a town. Precision-guided munitions fell by the ton on a little town 'til every shack, every mosque and shithouse where people lived their tortured camel-shit lives got turned to dust and wind 'cause of me. After the bombs stopped falling a place that used to be on a map got de-mapped from earth and that happened 'cause they pissed off an American soldier. They pissed off the man in your bed.

(Gabriela goes to Benito. She holds him, kisses him.)

GABRIELA: Oh, my baby . . . I just think it's better . . . you let this out of you . . . you won't be hunted in your sleep by the death of your friend no more . . .

(Benito looks at Gabriela.)

BENITO: What death?
GABRIELA: Your corporal. You must've lost your shit when he died. No wonder you—
BENITO: Uhm—he didn't *die*, Gabby.
GABRIELA: He didn't? What do you mean he—?
BENITO: Got *wounded* is what.
GABRIELA: Like—fatal-wounded? Lots of blood?
BENITO: His hand.
GABRIELA: Got blown off?
BENITO: Motherfuckers blew off his fingers!
GABRIELA: Wait a minute. A village in Iraq for a—?
BENITO: Very important fingers!
GABRIELA: You leveled it 'cause one of your buddies got a *pinky* wound?
BENITO: We evacuated them *first*, Gabby.
GABRIELA: You let them out before the bombs fell?
BENITO: *Most* of them anyway.
GABRIELA: *Some* people stayed and died?

BENITO: Ones that didn't *listen*—

GABRIELA: Women and children?—

BENITO: I can't control what happens in the mind of a raghead. Did they go? Some did. Others not. In a war . . .

GABRIELA: Which was over, you said.

BENITO: In a Rural Pacification Program . . .

GABRIELA: I hate your job. I really do. That's all I'm saying here.

BENITO: Swear, *nena,* you are unlimited in your ballbusting gifts! I'm trained to respond. What could I do?

GABRIELA: Not call the air strike?

BENITO: You weren't there. You don't know. We didn't know. We were in a *situation,* Gabby, blood, tension, enemies, heat, howling pain, adrenaline surge could give the Vatican a hard-on . . .

GABRIELA: You never do shit like that.

BENITO: It bothers you, we'll call an army shrink.

GABRIELA: Is it crazy if I don't like to think of you as a killer? If I don't like when they take my husband and make him kill?

BENITO: *Way* outta line, private—

GABRIELA: You hate it, too! You do! *Inside* you do! If you didn't, you wouldn't cry every time you close your eyes—

BENITO: *Coño,* man, you say, *este,* let's communicate—I say okay, let me give you every growling demon inside me making all the noise that keeps me up at night—*then* I say: girl, kill this fucker, 'cause I can't, bury this creature 'cause it's torturing me, and you put on fangs and torture me some more.

GABRIELA: You don't sound tortured. You sound proud you erased a town and wrote your name in its dust—but I don't believe it. I think it's a lie you tell yourself so you can survive the army.

BENITO: Sure about that? Maybe I liked watching the bombs fall.

GABRIELA: Don't say that—you didn't like it, Benito.

BENITO: Fine! I'm boycotting telling you anything serious anymore!

(Benito gets out of bed and straightens up the room, sweeping, etc.)

GABRIELA: That's cool 'cause you know what I did when you went to war I boycotted telling you about?

BENITO: You had an affair with an Iraqi.

GABRIELA: I had an affair with a guy named Muhammad.

BENITO: That better be an allegory of speech.

GABRIELA: I took a class in Bamholder on Arabs. I read about Islam. I didn't know jack about those people, but I thought—

BENITO: Hey. How do you clear an Iraqi bingo room? Yell: "B-52."

GABRIELA: I thought, He's going out to kill them, then I wanna know who they are. I learned about this orphan Muhammad, who believed in Jesus and humility and created a kneeling prayer 'cause his people were too proud to kneel to their God and he thought that was bullshit. An angel grabbed him by the nuts and said, "Recite!" And he recited and didn't stop for twenty years and practically invented his people's language when he did.

BENITO: I'm getting your library card burned on national television and the country will cheer.

GABRIELA: I thought—if I learned something about those people you're dropping "precision-guided munitions" on, I could respect them, and my respect, maybe, would balance out what you were doing, in a Karma way.

BENITO: A Karma way. Giving aid and comfort to the enemy—

GABRIELA: Nobody got any aid or comfort as I thought of you risking your ass for nothing.

BENITO: Freedom ain't nothing!

GABRIELA: How do you bomb a town to make it free?

BENITO: It's *over*, you fucking hippie! Good guys won. Good guys come home. Good guys pick up where they left off.

GABRIELA: It's never over. Spoken or not, a soldier takes his battles with him everywhere he goes. You taught me that.

BENITO: Not tonight, no. Tonight we're exempted from all shit. Tonight nothing gets through to us.

(Benito gets back into bed and kisses Gabriela.)

GABRIELA: Benny, I'm not trying to bust your balls . . . I just wish I had the words . . . for all the *thinking* I've been . . .

BENITO: At the edge of the bed, the soldier is just a man again.

(Before she can stop him, Benito pulls Gabriela closer.)

Tonight we're taking inventory. Reading all the pages on this fine book of photographs. Maybe we'll remember why we're here. What's this?

(Benito points to a scar on Gabriela's knee. It's an old game of theirs.)

GABRIELA: That was the morning I fell off the roof of my house playing Super Puerto Rican Girl with *Boricua* Power and I caught the corner of a fridge we kept outside, with my knee.

BENITO: A beautiful jagged mess. Like your mind. This?

(Benito kisses the scar and points to another on her thigh.)

GABRIELA: That was the afternoon my brother thought it'd be radically cute to plunge a fish hook bone-deep in my thigh. Repeatedly.

BENITO: Remind me to remove his entire thorax. This?

(Benito kisses the scar and touches another on her arm.)

GABRIELA: The night *Abuela* thought it'd be a howling pisser to stick the burning butt end of a Marlboro here and see how high I'd jump.
BENITO: Serious need for a lobotomy, that bearded old *bruja*-bitch, for hurting you in any way, shape or form. That's my real job. To hurt what hurts you.

(Benito sees a scar he's never seen before.)

What's this?
GABRIELA: Oh. Mexican kid next door asked me to play touch football and I slipped and cut myself.
BENITO: He changed your body! Who said your body's supposed to change, huh?

(Benito starts to kiss Gabriela.)

GABRIELA: Poor Benito's old lady keeps changing on him . . . can't even remember to keep a cold beer in the house . . . a pain in his very nice ass. Why do you put up with it, *Negro*?

(Gabriela kisses him deep. Surprised, not daring to hope for too much, he kisses her again. She responds quickly—covering him in hungry kisses, her hands and legs around and around him.

They make love. It's fast, rough and raw, a little desperate—finally climaxed by silence. Gabriela lies on her back, staring at the ceiling. Benito lies next to her, eyes closed. Gabriela quietly starts to cry. She doesn't want him to hear, so she tries to cover it, but he hears and reaches for her.

Gabriela quickly gets out of bed. She puts on jeans, a T-shirt and shoes. Benito watches her, motionless.)

BENITO: You still going to that class?

GABRIELA *(Shaking her head no)*: I'm leaving. You.

BENITO: You're leaving. Me.

(Gabriela packs clothes.)

GABRIELA: I have some money from Costco I saved up, I'll take the little car, I'll live in Victorville, or Los Angeles or Vegas. I don't really know at this . . .

BENITO: You only think you're leaving me.

GABRIELA: I ain't slept in that bed since you left for the field—

BENITO: Come back in the bed, please.

GABRIELA: —for two months I slept in the backyard, half-hoping those coyotes'd eat me.

(Benito gets out of bed and grabs Gabriela roughly.)

BENITO: The fuck you're leaving! Let's see you leave if I don't let you.

GABRIELA *(Pushing back)*: Don't push me, okay?

BENITO: You got somebody else? Little La Raza boy-toy next door?

GABRIELA: Please. Don't be stupid.

BENITO: Friggin' great news, Gab!

GABRIELA: I thought, No, I can't leave while you're in the field—you come home to an empty house—so out of *fairness,* I'll make you see I'm drowning in the sand and the cold—

BENITO: Swear, you use words like some people use razor wire and guard dogs.

GABRIELA: And maybe you'd see it, clearly—*finally*—and you'd decide, for me, for my fucking life, *leave* the army, turn your back on this deadly shit, and I could finally see what it's like to be married to you in a different way . . .

BENITO: When did you put on all these clothes I never seen before?

GABRIELA: . . . Not in an army town, where everybody's armed like the end of the world. Not smelling like tank fuel. Not playing God. Not one of us living a life the other can't understand anymore. But it's never gonna happen is it? —

BENITO: No—there's no—there's no . . . No! No! No!

GABRIELA: No! 'Cause the army's got you by the balls. And you like it! I'll tell you something—I'll share many things, I *do* share many things—but I won't share your balls! Not anymore!

BENITO: One total messed-up mental case . . .

GABRIELA: And who wouldn't get like that? The Ass of Heaven's got no real education 'cept what she scrapes together from night schools. Got no life-long friends. Got no experience but friggin' temp work 'cause of all our moving. I'd like to actually maybe be something some day better than working at Costco all my life. I'd like to make more than minimum wage before I'm thirty-eight. If you could just—listen—walk away from this life, *mi cielo*, and I know that would be so hard for you . . .

BENITO: You can't decide shit like this in secret.

GABRIELA: Imagine for me, *Negro*: us two making up other ways to be, where people wear clothes instead of uniforms, and nobody salutes nobody . . .

BENITO: This some kind of gruesome test?

GABRIELA: . . . And maybe we can both go back to school . . .

BENITO: Me and school? Are you cracked? I read at a fourth-grade level, you wanna know the absolute.

GABRIELA: I'll teach you to read better. I can do that. It don't kill your manhood to learn something from your wife, Benito. *Coño*, man . . . I . . . I grew up thinking I was stupid—but now? I know on planet Neptune, it rains dia-

monds. I know the moon's core is crystal—when it's hit
by an asteroid, the moon rings like a fucking bell!

BENITO: You're leaving 'cause I don't read books enough?
Don't know about Buddha and Allah and Salvador Dalí?

GABRIELA *(Not taking the bait)*: I tried so hard to love what you
love, see the purpose in it, to hate your enemies, I mean
really hate them. But I can't anymore, man; I can't fake
it . . . now, maybe, if you could love what I love . . .

BENITO: You think I'm common, but I'm not. I jump out of
planes. I climb mountains. I swim the ocean. I know mar-
tial arts. I can survive in the middle of nowhere with noth-
ing but shoestring and a mirror. I can take apart an M-16
A2 and put it back together blindfolded. I speak three lan-
guages. I met the secretary of defense. I defended an
oppressed country against naked *aggression*. I was in his-
tory. Is none of that any good anymore?

GABRIELA: And me? I followed you all over the earth. Lived
in lonely little towns where I hadda learn to say, *"Wo kann
man Reis und Bohnen kaufen?"*

BENITO *(Correcting her pronunciation)*: *Wo kann man Reis
und . . .*

GABRIELA: Where old German ladies looked at me like I just
dropped napalm on their babies. Oh, and then nobody in
the South can tell if I'm black or white. Everywhere—
stuck with left-behind wives who hated me.

BENITO: *Nena*—please—I know you had it bad. Sacrifices
every fucking day—thank you, thank you, and thank
you—but're you really saying you got nothing back?

GABRIELA: I'm not talking *things* . . .

BENITO: You had parents wanted to haul your ass to Alcatraz.
You had intimate knowledge of the juvenile *penal* system,
when we met.

GABRIELA: Uh-huh, uh-huh, when we met—yeah—your
uniform had stars on it. But then, *mi amor*—the stars on

the uniform started to fade. God, why didn't I say something years ago?

BENITO: A home, protection from the sun, a car, lots of eats, love, you get love, because I stupidly, ridiculously, fanatically love you—you get that?—you see that in the plus column? Should I repeat? It's the love, stupid!

GABRIELA: Please don't throw that word around like a fucking hand grenade . . .

BENITO: I'm sorry I love you *and* the army. I'm sorry I have two loves. But one, you might notice, is inanimate. Ain't got a soul. Can't really compete.

GABRIELA: It's doing not so bad, I think!

BENITO: What you really want is for me to like literally attach myself surgically to the hip.

GABRIELA: It'd be, like, an improvement—

BENITO: Well, here's the big *Geraldo* news flash, *nena*: one hundred percent of me? Not available in any store. Why? 'Cause I need to be—don't even think of laughing—some place, whatever, that's my privacy: where you can't go.

GABRIELA: This just in: I know.

BENITO: I get that private thing in the field sometimes. When I'm out there, I can feel—all the previous wars. Feel them in my body. My chest. No wonder that's where they put the medals. Out there training, before they stuck my ass in Star Wars, I tried to even feel, you know, Korea in me, even Vietnam. Men doing impossible things together. Men agreeing.

GABRIELA: Men, men, men . . . with no room left over for women and children . . .

BENITO: With codes and rules on how to be. Instead of all the chaos puked on the world by eunuchs—all pussy-whipped—worried about exchange rates, big weekend warriors, playing their mind games on the weak like there was no absolutes for valor and manhood and freedom.

GABRIELA: You joined the army 'cause you were poor.

BENITO: And I ain't poor no more. And I don't mean the Grand National parked outside. I mean in me, my mind. The war on poverty ended and I won it.

GABRIELA: Who's prouder of you than me? I just think— you're only using half or a tenth or a millionth of this great, beautiful mind you run away from like the plague . . .

BENITO: Did I hallucinate all the nights we had together? Taking long baths, playing cards with our friends, you drinking beers, telling dirty jokes, your hand on my knee, big, big laughter. Sometimes you looked me in the eye, the tears falling, fat as snakes, your fingers around my stick so tight you almost broke it, eyes on fire, you whisper so low and sexy, "I love you, baby,"—you said that!—"so much, I want to have eight kids with you." The pants come down. The legs get wrapped around my neck. Do I not believe that now? Was it a lie? Are you lying now? Were you crazy then? Are you crazy now?

GABRIELA: I was eighteen when I said that about the babies. With a big mouth and dreams. Long before we knew I was fixed and God was playing tricks with my body. Before the war changed you.

BENITO: The war didn't change me. It changed you.

GABRIELA: Fucking right it changed me. Every single day for a year . . . glued like a mummy to the TV . . . watching CNN, looking at all the American soldiers—going, Is that him? Is he eating okay? Does he look happy? No, it's not him. I don't see him. Don't see my Benito. So I turn the TV off and lie on the floor—and imagine you as a P.O.W.—who they take apart and put back together any old way they fucking feel like it. Oh—and night wasn't any better, 'cause of the dreams.

(Beat.)

In my dream: I get your body after the war. You can't move. I can't figure out why. You open your mouth for me. I put my hand down your throat. My whole arm goes in. Your skin is see-through so I watch my hand groping the things in your stomach. There's little round rocks in you, smooth, like from a beach, and I pull these outta your stomach by the fistful but you don't get better. Not 'til I'm reaching deeper in your bowels and pull out the rusted nails and burning bits of shrapnel that were in there and they cut my hand to pieces but I don't stop until I pull them all out of your body.

(Beat.)

BENITO: Do I get better?

GABRIELA: Never know. I wake up.

BENITO: Don't wanna end up married to a cripple, who could blame you? . . .

GABRIELA: If you came home that way—I'd take care of you. For the rest of your life. No questions asked. But it has to be you. The man I met and loved . . .

BENITO *(Losing his patience)*: Christ, Gab, you make it sound like the war's turned me into some kind of animal. Look at these hands. They don't just pull triggers and evaporate life. They have other jobs besides counting dead. These are good hands. You know that. You know I can fix every bad dream in your head. I can cure this insanity you have . . .

GABRIELA: What if I can't forget so easy? What if I can't get the dead women and children off your hands? What if I feel them every time you touch me?

BENITO: *Nena, Dios,* that's fucked what you're saying—

GABRIELA: It's gotta be said—I gotta know: are you inside there? All you did was come home from work. Me? I'm digging up my husband from the grave—looking for the lover I had before the world sucked out his mind and heart . . .

BENITO: You don't deserve to have a house. You don't deserve security.

GABRIELA: *Coño,* that is so lame it's not even—

BENITO: Oh fuck it, fuck it! Man, what is wrong with me? Standing in this bedroom begging you to stay with me? I don't have to beg no damn woman for no damn thing in the world. You have *assaulted* me with this shit. You've hit me right between the eyes, *nena.* It'd be better to just take my sidearm and let the bullets do the talking. I don't beg. A man does not beg. You go find what you're missing. Read every book in the world. 'Cause right now we're "like" oil and water, we're "like" a train wreck, and you know what? Thank you, baby. This was good. Saved us a lot of time. I now have more time to watch TV.

(Benito puts on his clothes.)

GABRIELA: What are you doing?

BENITO: You know what? You're wrong—I don't run from my mind, I don't, I live inside myself, where there's no way out, and I see what I do. I see what I put you through, for years.

GABRIELA: Could this be a whiff of a hint of a shadow of saying: "I understand"?

BENITO: Just, please, forgive me and hold on until I can retire in nine years. You can do it, private. The war was a fluke. There will not be another one in my life. I'll do everything I can to get orders for any place on earth but Germany or the desert. I'll volunteer for Star Wars. I'll suck off the captain. I'll learn to type. Just don't make me rip my life in half and erase eleven years of it— 'cause then I'm dead for sure, Gabby.

GABRIELA *(Grateful)*: Why do you gotta be that way?

BENITO: 'Cause I'm not supposed to make it easy for you to break my heart.

GABRIELA: Like I made it easy for you? I'll make it harder. I'll stay in the army life for you, nine years, if that's what . . . but you gotta . . . I don't know if I even know . . . I got so many words in my head and when I need them, they fuck with me . . . it's like this . . . uhm, it's like, like . . .

(She's run out of words. Benito looks at her with pity and incomprehension.)

BENITO: I'm gone. I'll be on post. You decide if you wanna be here when I come home tomorrow morning. We'll try the homecoming again, if you want. But really think about it. Think about me. Don't do anything until you think about me.

(Benito leaves the room. Gabriela collapses onto the bed. She thinks about everything.
Coyotes howl.
Gabriela falls asleep. Blackout.)

⚜ ACT FOUR ⚜

Early morning.

Lights up on the backyard. A hint of sunlight over the east threatens the darkness.

The Moon is faint, weak, low in the sky, softly playing the violin. Martín and Gabriela, not touching, sleep side by side. Cat watches Gabriela sleep. Martín wakes up.

MARTÍN *(To the Moon)*:
> After my pistol of love
> found its target and
> exploded with love-shrapnel
> inside her, and sent her mind
> to the dizzy edge of the universe,
> where it sat and wondered
> what the fuck hit it . . .
> she fell asleep.
> Mission accomplished!
> I am now a man.
> Other men notice my manhood
> and are suddenly afraid.

MOON *(Bored, sarcastic)*:
. . . *So hide your daughters, people.*

MARTÍN:
So hide your daughters, people!

(Gabriela wakes up.)

GABRIELA:
I just had the strangest dream . . .

MARTÍN:
I think I got you pregnant.

GABRIELA:
*Then you have the only sperm
on earth that crawls across cement,
burrows through cotton panties,
and grows flowers in barren sand.*

MARTÍN:
Ask the moon what I did!

MOON *(Weak)*:
*At night, love can't
hide from me.
My light penetrates.
When virgin blood and
virgin seed hit the sheets,
I'm there,
counting the droplets.
Last night? Zero.*

GABRIELA *(To the Moon)*:
Delightful job you have.

MOON *(Weak)*:
> *It's a living.*
> *But, now, my time is almost over.*
> *Gotta go to bed.*
> *My sister the sun is*
> *impatient and pushy.*

GABRIELA:
> *In my dream: cats don't talk.*
> *Refrigerators are indoor appliances.*
> *The moon doesn't play the violin.*
> *On the moon, sunlight cooks the land*
> *and there's zero romance and no sound.*
> *Dreams don't get born there.*
> *Some day the moon will be landfill,*
> *people think.*
> *So the moon watches,*
> *with indifference,*
> *as the earth rises*
> *out of its bleached horizon,*
> *all soft and blue,*
> *like a marble covered in tears.*

(The Moon yawns, gets dimmer.)

MOON:
> *Yeah, whatever.*

GABRIELA:
> *But what if I'm still dreaming?*
> *What if none of us wake up?*
> *What if we go on like this:*
> *dreaming and sleeping,*
> *until we're like boxes-within-boxes*
> *and there's no way out?*

MOON:

> Adios, *Gabby!*

GABRIELA *(To the Moon):*

> Before you go, explain my dream to me.
> I couldn't recognize Benito and me.

MOON:

> That was a dream about soul mates.

GABRIELA:

> Who never agree? Who misinterpret?

MOON:

> You two go deep.
> So the wounds go deep.
> You give a person so much,
> you rearrange them.
> You rewrite them.
> He's your creation.
> You're his.

GABRIELA:

> Was it all a mistake?
> Was it all hormones
> and sweaty fingers?
> Beer and pot and sucking each other?
> Was it the uniform?
> Was it the jokes he told
> and the food he cooked?
> Was it just youth?
> Why didn't I take more pictures
> of those days?
> Why can't I remember
> them better?

MOON *(Weak)*:
> *Too tired to think . . .*

GABRIELA:
> *Who wouldn't get married*
> *under those circumstances?*
> *Who wouldn't assume*
> *that passion—and tenderness—*
> *could last forever?*
> *Who could have predicted*
> *the changes in the body and the spirit?*

(The Moon starts to set.)

MOON *(Fading)*:
> *. . . Don't turn to me*
> *for precise answers, Gabby . . .*
> *I'm a reflection of a reflection . . .*
> *I'm a codependent satellite . . .*
> *not even confident enough*
> *to be a planet . . .*
> *and what you ask about . . .*
> *are intangibles . . .*
> *there will always be things*
> *you can't know about each other . . .*
> *there has never been a machine*
> *made to X-ray the heart*
> *and reveal its secrets,*
> *except for poetry . . .*
> *and I'm way too tired*
> *to deal with poetry tonight . . .*
> *Shakespeare called me "inconstant" . . .*
> *"That monthly changes in her circled orb" . . .*
> *even got my gender wrong . . .*

the motherfucker . . .
but I guess I am . . .
that's as close to precise
as the moon can get . . .

MARTÍN *(To the Moon)*:
I wish you'd leave already!

MOON *(To Gabriela)*:
Think. Be strong.
And be careful . . . everything you do
may seem like a mistake . . .
for a very long time to come . . .

(The Moon disappears. More sunlight.)

GABRIELA *(To Martín)*:
Boy, you need to go.

MARTÍN:
But I'm your man.
And you stole my virginity.
You owe me something for that.

GABRIELA:
Sun's coming up.
Benito comes home from the field
this morning, seven a.m.,
must be close to that,
I suggest you disappear, muchacho.

MARTÍN:
I'm only saying
I want to spoil you—
on a cellular level.

GABRIELA:

    Child, I'd break you in two.

MARTÍN:

    Then give me back my virginity.

GABRIELA:

    I'll give you back your virginity.

    (Gabriela kisses Martín passionately.)

MARTÍN:

    The giving was better than the taking!

GABRIELA:

    You're a sweet kid, Martín.
    You don't belong in Barstow, either.
    We have that in common.
    You kiss good.

MARTÍN *(To Cat)*:

    I kiss good.

GABRIELA:

    I can see going crazy in your bed
    and burning your house to the ground
    with the two of us
    taking long baths together
    and drinking so much beer
    we'd both have comas for a week.

MARTÍN:

    I'm searching for the downside
    to all this.

GABRIELA:

> *I can see you getting*
> *more and more dangerous, Martín.*
> *I can tell by looking in your eyes:*
> *you're the type*
> *that falls in love real easy.*
> *That plans babies*
> *after the first conversation.*
> *Like somebody I*
> *fell in love with*
> *when I wasn't much*
> *older than you.*

MARTÍN:

> *You think . . . other girls*
> *see the same danger as you?*

GABRIELA:

> *You broadcast it through your eyes.*

MARTÍN:

> *Are you saying I'll never get laid?*

GABRIELA:

> *Not with me,* muchachito.

(Martín looks at Gabriela, angry; it's as if his entire personality has changed.)

MARTÍN:

> *I gotta go.*
> *This whole thing is bullshit!*
> *And I don't want any more of you*
> *playing with my head,*

you cutting my nuts off,
*you doing psycho-*brujeria-*witchcraft on me.*
I'm glad we never got involved—bitch!
I'm glad I broke your heart!

GABRIELA:

Did I miss something here? . . .

(Martín starts to climb over the yard's fence.)

MARTÍN:

Oh sure, you look at Martín—
ay, he's so cute,
those chubby cheeks make me hot—
but you don't know.
Before I met you, all I thought about
was renting porn, shooting coyotes
at night, and taking target practice
on the moon.
You made me think new thoughts!
If I have to face manhood without you—
will the world crush me?
If I don't touch a woman's thing,
like really soon,
will I finally go berserk
and blow you all away?
Or will my explosions
happen so deep inside
no one will feel them but me?

(He is gone. Gabriela sadly thinks about him, the Moon and Benito: all the men in her life. The Cat looks at her worriedly.)

CAT *(To Gabriela)*:
> *You okay, nena?*

GABRIELA:
> *I don't know what I'm going to do*
> *to get ready for Benito.*

CAT:

> *You could have both*
> *your eyes sucked out of your face*
> *and replaced with the eyes*
> *of a teenage Persian slave girl.*

GABRIELA:
> *No. Did that.*

CAT:

> *You could change into*
> *Salvador Dalí's foreskin*
> *and fuck a red-haired soprano.*

GABRIELA:
> *No.*

CAT:

> *Or you could organize the red ants*
> *that live in the garage and*
> *teach them to milk each other*
> *so you never run out of milk*
> *for Benito's coffee.*

GABRIELA:
> *Yeah . . .*

CAT:

> *You could drink a hummingbird's saliva*
> *drop by little drop . . .*

GABRIELA:

> *. . . and stare into Benito's eyes*
> *and try to read his mind*
> *and wonder if we still*
> *love each other.*
> *And if I can't figure it out*
> *I think the thing I have to do*
> *is devise a gruesome test.*

CAT:

> *A gruesome test! I like that!*

GABRIELA:

> *The first night we met,*
> *there was a fight in a white-trash bar.*
> *Benito and other recruits*
> *were on the floor getting nailed*
> *by local skinheads.*
> *I pulled him to his feet*
> *and ran out of the bar with him*
> *before it really got ugly!*
> *As we ran from the bar*
> *into the night . . .*
> *there was a wicked moon in the sky,*
> *smoking a Cuban cigar,*
> *playing a mandolin with*
> *thirteen-and-a-half strings.*
> *Benito stopped to look at the moon.*
> *The skinheads were gaining on us.*

He said it looked so cool tonight.
I didn't even notice it
and he made me notice it.
I realized I like a man who notices
the moon even with skinheads
coming closer and closer.
I thought that was brave and thoughtful . . .
I thought that was manly and kind.
He asked me if I was an angel and
wondered if God would let him fuck me
if he was extra good around Christmas.
I was fifteen years old!
And I took him as far from virginity
as you can get.
And for a while,
we were each other's
drugs and cigarettes.
We floated in and out of dreams
that both of us wrote . . .
I can forgive everything
if I know for sure
he's the same man I saved from peril.
So I'll ask him about last night.
Did he see last night's moon
or has he stopped looking
at the sky forever?

(The sound of a car entering the house's garage.)

CAT:

Guess who.

(Gabriela opens the refrigerator. It's full of sand.)

GABRIELA *(Nervous)*:
> *Outta milk!*
> *I'm getting weird déjà vu.*
> *Got nothing clean to wear*
> *but these shorts.*

CAT:
> *He'll see you like that*
> *and think: horny housewife.*

GABRIELA:
> *This can't be like other times.*
> *I have to think about Benito.*
> *I have to make him see*
> *we could be looking*
> *at a train wreck . . .*

> *(Coyote's Ghost enters the backyard. Cat gasps, smiles.)*

CAT:
> *Nena, wait! What do I do*
> *if my lover's a ghost?*

GABRIELA:
> *Fuck him anyway, Cat.*

> *(Gabriela moves off by herself, waiting for Benito.*
> *Coyote's Ghost and Cat stare at each other in wonder.)*

CAT *(To Coyote's Ghost)*:
> *I thought you were dead, Coyote.*

COYOTE'S GHOST *(To the Cat)*:
> *I'm a ghost.*

CAT:

> I thought I'd never see you again.

COYOTE'S GHOST:

> I'm a memory.

CAT:

> A vivid one—my body remembers!
> A difficult one too.

COYOTE'S GHOST:

> I'm a dream.
> I'm not really here.

CAT:

> I know. I miss you.

COYOTE'S GHOST:

> You were right not to trust me.
> I wanted to hurt you.
> To teach you to be wild.
> Then kill you quick—
> and eat you
> and not give a shit.

CAT:

> When the moonlight stabbed you
> and ripped you off,
> all my hopes for a wild ride
> in the endless night seemed to end.
> But you're back!

COYOTE'S GHOST:

> Why do you stare at me?

CAT:

> *You're transparent!*
> *It's so cool!*

COYOTE'S GHOST:

> *I can't even smell you.*

CAT:

> *Coyote, I'm hot.*

COYOTE'S GHOST:

> *I can't smell anything.*
> *What kind of hunter will I be?*

CAT:

> *Smell me and you'll know.*

COYOTE'S GHOST:

> *My appetite for blood: gone!*

CAT:

> *There are other kinds of smells.*
> *Other kinds of hunger.*
> *An infinity of tastes.*
> *And ways to satisfy.*

COYOTE'S GHOST:

> *Show me what you mean . . .*

> *(Cat approaches Coyote's Ghost and breathes deeply.)*

CAT:

> *¡Ay! You smell like air!*
> *You smell—like heaven,*

> *like a graveyard on a cloudy day.*
> *You smell like transformation, hope, prayers.*
> *You smell like a whisper.*

COYOTE'S GHOST:

> *What are you thinking, Cat?*

CAT:

> *Thoughts! Wild ones!*

COYOTE'S GHOST:

> *Do you trust me?*

CAT:

> *I trust you.*

COYOTE'S GHOST:

> *How long will I last with you?*

CAT:

> *Before we lose our courage?*

COYOTE'S GHOST:

> *How long do I really have?*

CAT:

> *Before the deceptions start?*

COYOTE'S GHOST:

> *And the fights to the death.*

CAT:

> *And the madness.*

COYOTE'S GHOST:
> *How long can we possibly last?*

CAT:

> *Before we have to test*
> *each other's love?*

(Cat and Coyote's Ghost approach each other. They dance.)

BENITO'S VOICE:
> *Where are you?*

GABRIELA:

> *In the backyard.*
> *I slept here last night.*

(Benito enters the backyard.)

BENITO:
> *Something wrong with the bed?*

GABRIELA:
> *I just did, that's all.*

BENITO:
> *Is there any coffee?*

GABRIELA:
> *You lost a lot of weight.*

BENITO:
> *God bless that army food.*

GABRIELA:
    And nice circles under the eyes.

BENITO:
    Ain't slept in forty-eight hours.

GABRIELA:
    You don't like my haircut . . .

BENITO:
    Makes you look older—
    but not too much—
    five or six years at the most!

GABRIELA:
    Here's your gun.

BENITO:
    Don't say "gun"—it's a "weapon."
    Your gun hangs between your legs.

GABRIELA:
    Nothing hangs between my legs, soldier-boy.

BENITO:
    Except for me. Gabby.
    My cute, smart, sexy,
    totally hot Gabby . . .

GABRIELA:
    I have a question.
    It's going to sound stupid,
    but I have to ask you.
    Did you see the moon last night?

BENITO:
. . . better than pogey bait . . .

GABRIELA:
Did you see the moon last night?
I really have to know this, Benito.
I really have to know.

(Lights fade to black as Gabriela awaits Benito's answer.
Cat and Coyote's Ghost dance slow and hot and tight.)

END OF PLAY

SUEÑO

ADAPTED FROM
PEDRO CALDERÓN DE LA BARCA'S
Life Is a Dream

For Adena and Teo

SPECIAL THANKS TO

Patrick Egan, Richard Riehle,
Ben Siegler, Zillah Hill, Sab Shimono,
Gregory Wallace and Maria Canals

PRODUCTION HISTORY

Sueño was commissioned by Hartford Stage Company (Mark Lamos, Artistic Director) and developed with the assistance of the Mark Taper Forum (Gordon Davidson, Artistic Director).

Sueño received its world premiere at the Hartford Stage Company (Michael Wilson, Artistic Director; Stephen J. Albert, Managing Director) in Hartford, Connecticut, on February 20, 1998. The world premiere production was sponsored by Aetna, The Hartford Foundation for Public Giving and the National Endowment for the Arts. It was directed by Lisa Peterson; scenic design was by Michael Yeargan, costume design was by Meg Neville, lighting design was by Christopher Akerlind, sound design was by David Budries, fight direction was by David Leong, the dramaturg was Morgan Jenness and the production stage manager was Deborah Vandergrift. The cast was as follows:

BASILIO	Geno Silva
DON CLOTALDO	Yusef Bulos
SERVANT	Ken Parker
ROSAURA	Michi Barall
CLARÍN	Jan Leslie Harding
SEGISMUNDO	John Ortiz
ASTOLFO	Damian Young
ESTRELLA	Alene Dawson
IST SOLDIER	Sam Wellington

GUARDS, SERVANTS,
   SOLDIERS, REBELS   Darin Dunston, John Socas

Sueño received its New York premiere at MCC Theater (Robert LuPone and Bernard Telsey, Artistic Directors; William Cantler, Associate Artistic Director) by special arrangement with Hartford Stage Company on March 1, 2000. It was directed by Lisa Peterson; scenic design was by Riccardo Hernandez, costume design was by Anita Yavich, lighting design was by Christopher Akerlind, original music and sound design were by Fabian Obispo, original guitar music was by Aaron Gilmartin, flamenco instruction was by Gloria Marina, fight direction was by Rick Sordelet, the production manager was Rob Conover and the production stage manager was Lisa Gavaletz. The cast was as follows:

BASILIO	Geno Silva
DON CLOTALDO	Yusef Bulos
SERVANT	Ken Parker
ROSAURA	Michi Barall
CLARÍN	David Greenspan
SEGISMUNDO	John Ortiz
ASTOLFO	James Urbaniak
ESTRELLA	Rebecca Wisocky
IST SOLDIER	Sam Wellington
GUARDS, SERVANTS, SOLDIERS, REBELS	Lorenzo Gregorio, Ken Parker, Jeremy J. H. Seymour, Sam Wellington

CHARACTERS

BASILIO, King of Spain.
DON CLOTALDO, his *valido*, Rosaura's father.
SERVANT
ROSAURA, a young woman from Poland.
CLARÍN, her manservant.
SEGISMUNDO, Prince of Spain, son of Basilio.
ASTOLFO, Duke of Warsaw.
ESTRELLA, a princess.
IST SOLDIER, a rebel leader.

Beauty will be convulsive—or will cease to be.

—ANDRÉ BRETON
"MANIFESTO OF SURREALISM, 1924"

He realized that, though he may penetrate all the riddles of the
higher and lower orders, the task of shaping the senseless and
dizzying stuff of dreams is the hardest that a man can
attempt—much harder than weaving a rope of sand or of
coining the faceless wind.

—JORGE LUIS BORGES
"THE CIRCULAR RUINS"

No es sueño la vida.

—FEDERICO GARCÍA LORCA
THE POETIC WORKS OF FEDERICO GARCÍA LORCA

⚔ ACT ONE ⚔

SCENE 1

Spain. 1610. King Basilio's palace. Midday. The sun and the moon are approaching total eclipse.

Basilio and his valido Don Clotaldo are in their forties. Basilio looks over sheets of parchment.

The distant, painful sound of a woman in labor.

BASILIO *(Reading the parchment)*: His horoscopes tell us he'll be born a monster.

DON CLOTALDO: And if the stars are wrong, Your Majesty? —

BASILIO: Wrong? The sun itself weeps blood. It fights for its life against a ferocious moon. See for yourself: it's the worst eclipse since the Crucifixion!

DON CLOTALDO: Coincidence, only.

BASILIO *(Not listening)*: Dark omens on the eve of his birth are everywhere. Buildings shake. Rocks fall from the clouds. Trees spontaneously burn. Night lasts forty-eight hours. And strange new constellations pollute the night sky with unreadable portents. Have you ever seen anything like it?

DON CLOTALDO: Only in my dreams.

BASILIO: Every astrologer in the kingdom predicts my child will grow up to be a cruel, tyrannical, and outrageous prince. He'll cut the kingdom in two in an endless and tragic civil war. He'll trample my dishonored corpse on his way to the throne.

DON CLOTALDO: But stars only point the way to the future, sire, they don't create it. They can bend the will but they can't force—

BASILIO: And last night the queen dreamed—

(The Servant enters carrying a baby wrapped in a bloody blanket.)

SERVANT: King Basilio. Your son.

BASILIO: The queen?

SERVANT: Dead.

BASILIO: Dead!

SERVANT: The boy burst through her body like a man-eating tiger, cutting her in half and severing her from the living world.

BASILIO: She's killed by her son! He's baptized in her blood! This thing is already a man, Clotaldo. It's repaid goodness with cruelty. Its first living act was murder. What do you say now?

DON CLOTALDO *(Taking the baby)*: He has your eyes, sire.

BASILIO: God of Love, how do I solve this? How do I rewrite this creature's destiny? How do I save Spain—and myself?

(Basilio exits. The baby cries.)

DON CLOTALDO *(To Servant)*: . . . Is there any milk in the castle?

(A total eclipse plunges the stage into darkness.)

SCENE 2

1635. A mountain. A tower. The tower door is open.

Rosaura, twenty-five, robust, clever, loud, dressed as a man, tumbles onto the stage, landing hard on her back. At her side is an ornate sword.

ROSAURA *(On her back, in pain)*: Violent, mixed-up horse! Unnaturally stupid mammal! Instinct-challenged freak!

(Rosaura picks herself up and yells at the offstage horse.)

If you were a bird you wouldn't know how to fly! If you were a stream you wouldn't know how to babble! You're a fart without smell! A religion without God! A dreamer without sleep!

(Clarín, her elderly manservant, enters, his fingers in his ears.)

CLARÍN: I see your lungs are still working, madam.

ROSAURA: Did you see that dumb beast throw me? Ran to the edge of the cliff. Something scared it—it stopped—and the momentum knocked me down the mountain so hard, it practically left me blind.

CLARÍN *(Looking)*: Good . . . otherwise you'd have to watch both our horses taking off.

ROSAURA *(Seeing it)*: Get back here! No, dammit! It's as if they know something about this dismal place.

CLARÍN: Maybe they're not as stupid as we look, huh?

ROSAURA: It's a fine age we live in—when horses no longer act like horses. Maps?

CLARÍN: In the saddlebags galloping back to Poland at, oh, fifty miles an hour.

ROSAURA (*Looking around*): Brilliant! Lost! Lost in some ugly desert . . . some freak frontier . . . look at it, Clarín: illogical stone formations, creepy craters. The place looks like the backside of the moon.

CLARÍN: Food, drink, and shelter would be nice, huh?

ROSAURA: You're a dreamer. Is it Spain? It looks vaguely Spanish: morbid and feisty all at the same time. Hey, Spain! Is this how you stamp the passport of each new immigrant to your country—in blood?

CLARÍN: Horseless, stranded, wronged, overburdened, screwed, molested, tampered with, addicted to stress . . .

ROSAURA: Sun's going down. Add "cold" to your list of miseries.

CLARÍN: Darkness! Ask yourself: what queer tricksters and fiends accompany the darkness of Castile? What contaminated mirage, I wonder, will come along to pick our pockets and flog our imaginations? I miss Poland! Our mad adventure is over, madam! We're doomed! Oh, fuck it, let's have a little sex before we die.

(*Clarín goes to embrace Rosaura. She easily pushes him away as she sees the tower.*)

ROSAURA: Either I've started dreaming or I've succumbed to hypnosis or I've been hit by the arrow of an aimless sorcerer . . . but in the sun's last shy rays, I see . . . I don't know what I see . . .

CLARÍN: I don't know either, but I see it, too.

ROSAURA: A palace? Too decrepit. A fortress? Too solitary. A home? Too unhappy.

CLARÍN: Prison. I know the smell.

ROSAURA: Yes, a prison carved into the stubborn architecture of the mountain—camouflaged by walls of rock. A labyrinth so well hidden the sun's perfect eyesight has no way of seeing it. Recommendation?

CLARÍN: A closer look. Let's give the owners a chance to wine and dine a pair of starving hobos.

ROSAURA: How do I look?

CLARÍN: Manly, madam—sir!

ROSAURA *(Approaching the tower)*: That door . . . looks more like a wound than a door. Or it's the deep uterus out of which midnight's darkness itself is born. Or the cave from which nightmares enter the world of the sleeping . . .

(The sound of chains.)

CLARÍN: Chains of a prisoner? A slave? Or a ghost?

SEGISMUNDO'S VOICE: *¡Ay misero de mi! ¡Ay infelice!*

CLARÍN: It's a baby's cry!

ROSAURA: A poor unborn man crying from his cradle of stone.

CLARÍN: Rosaura, I'd like to leave this hoodoo place! I know this pitiful cry means nothing but tricks and suffering and really really bad bad torments.

(A weak light appears at the door. Rosaura looks in.)

ROSAURA: A brief, doubtful light . . . shows me a dark habitat . . . and Clarín!—the ghost of a poor man—no, more reflection than ghost, a walking mirage, born dead, dressed in animal skins . . . a slave, maybe, stolen from the oppressed Indies, or a refugee of a defeated warrior-state where nightmares are rulers and Aztec monsters walk the streets.

CLARÍN: Poor thing. His only companion is the exhausted light and the dead silence of the mountains.

ROSAURA: And us.

(Segismundo, twenty-five, a wild man dressed in animal skins, arms and legs bound with long chains, holding a lantern, appears in the tower.)

SEGISMUNDO: God of Love, God of Light, are you listening? If you exist, tell me: what law have I broken today? What have I done to deserve this punishment? Your books tell me that birth is a sin. I was born once, I think. Am I being punished for my original sin? But—aren't *all men* born with this sin? Aren't all men guilty? And if all are guilty of the strange crime of being born shouldn't *all men* be enslaved as I am? Yet, I know from my small experience of the world that some men are actually free. Free! Yet here I am! Why? What's so different about me? Birds are free. Birds are beautiful. Is it their beauty that exempts them? I've never seen my face. Am I un-free because I am un-beautiful? And wild snakes are ugly! Yet they are free! It isn't mere ugliness, then, that imprisons me, it's something else. My ugliness goes deep. It's an ugliness of the soul. An ugliness so contagious, God is afraid I'll infect the body of the world. That's why I must be quarantined—like a secret medical experiment—God's wild new virus kept under strict control. I am the soul of polio and anthrax! Yet even now . . . in this degenerate state . . . why should I, a man made vaguely in God's image . . . why should I, who have more soul and better instincts and greater will and more life than a bird or a wild snake or a simple germ . . . why should I be less free?

ROSAURA *(Sotto voce, to Clarín)*: Those unhappy words break my heart.

SEGISMUNDO: Who's out there? Who's listening to me? Don Clotaldo?

CLARÍN *(Sotto voce, to Rosaura)*: Say yes and don't tell him about me!

(Rosaura steps forward. Clarín remains hidden.)

ROSAURA: A poor traveler—forlorn and dishonored like yourself . . .

(Segismundo hurls himself at Rosaura. She goes for her sword. He disarms her. He holds her, covers her eyes with one hand and squeezes. Rosaura screams.)

SEGISMUNDO: I'll tear your eyes from your head for having seen too much of the world and too much of me!

CLARÍN *(Hidden)*: I'm a blind old ghost and I haven't seen a thing!

ROSAURA *(Struggling)*: If you were indeed born a man and not a monster—I know all I have to do is kneel before you and you'll give me mercy.

(Segismundo lets go of Rosaura's face. Holding her, Segismundo explores Rosaura's body. He sniffs her.)

SEGISMUNDO: Your voice . . . is that what they call "melody"? Your face . . . is that what they mean by "art"? Are women and oceans this beautiful? These are your eyes. There's light in them . . . is that what the stars look like when seen by a free man? Your confusing skin . . . it's human skin . . . not the cold iron of the Inquisitor. Blow!

(Segismundo holds his hand in front of Rosaura's mouth and she blows.)

Is that like the wind? Is that a hurricane? Is that the rain? Say your name.

ROSAURA: I can't.

SEGISMUNDO *(Laughs)*: It doesn't matter. Your curses would sound to me like the opening notes of Creation. In the Beginning were the words: "I can't."

(Segismundo presses his thumbs into her throat.)

ROSAURA: Sir! No!

(He stops.)

SEGISMUNDO: This box is my crib and my grave. This sewer pipe is all I've ever known of life. I've been nothing but a bag of guts, a storm of chemical responses pretending to have a soul, eating and shitting and waiting to die! All this time I've spoken to one person. A dark man whose face I've never seen. Don Clotaldo gives me advice—he tells me how to hold my dick so I don't piss on myself! He tries to describe women to me! And courtship. And violin playing. And government. And honor. He tells me of the wonders of an Eden discovered beyond the Ocean Sea. I dream some day I'll be exiled to that New World, to live among my kind, the noble savages at one with nature, on pure land ten times the size of Europe! My grim teacher hears all my thoughts. He's my silent diary, taking in all my dreams, my confessions and worries. He teaches me to read the Bible! He tells me, there, between the lines, there is the flickering light, the shining residue of God's glory. God's actual fingerprints are there in the space between Psalms, between the screaming heartbeats of the suffering Christ on the cross. Yes! And I've learned my language by listening to those delicious words "glory," "grace," "resurrection," "redemption," gentle words that soothed my wrists and ankles when I was a boy like pure water poured on bloody wounds. Yes! But the years have passed so slowly. And that black book has taught me a world I would never see beyond this black box. One day I grabbed the book from Don Clotaldo and I tore its pages and put them in my mouth and I ate them. I ate them! Chapter and verse! I chewed those holy, phony sentiments, swallowed them whole, and shit them out again. I've been eating Bibles and shitting Gospels all my life. The words are written in my tissues now. In the blood vessels of my brain. In the hollow rooms of my mind, lining the walls with lies and promises!

(Segismundo grabs his head as if experiencing searing pain. As it subsides, he looks at Rosaura.)

Sir, your voice has quieted those cunning words. Your skin is the only texture these depleted fingers have ever enjoyed. My thirsty eyes know it's poison to drink you in—but they are dying to see that which will kill them to see. I don't care! Let me look at you—more natural than all the Nature I've seen fornicating from my narrow window—you, the gift of life—and let me die!

ROSAURA: My eyes and ears amaze me today. They show me wonders and tell me stories I've never seen or heard before. I don't know what to say—or what to ask first. All I know is this: today Heaven dropped me here and brought me comfort—if it's possible to be comforted by someone more desperate than yourself. I know my pain would be joy to you and you'd receive it gladly. If I can give you any comfort, sir, let me do it by telling you my own desperate story.

SEGISMUNDO: I sensed it! Someone has wronged you, sir. Someone has dishonored you.

ROSAURA: Yes, but the first thing to know about me is this: I am not a—

DON CLOTALDO'S VOICE *(From off)*: Guards! Careless, foolish guards!

CLARÍN *(Hidden)*: Great! More confusion!

ROSAURA: Who's that?

SEGISMUNDO: Don Clotaldo, my mentor and tormentor!

DON CLOTALDO'S VOICE *(Off)*: All intruders are to be arrested at once!

CLARÍN *(Hidden)*: My God, we're dead!

(Don Clotaldo and two Guards enter. Don Clotaldo wears a mask. The Guards carry masks and firearms.)

DON CLOTALDO *(To the Guards)*: Hide your faces!

(The Guards put on their masks.)

CLARÍN *(Hidden)*: Costume party with guns!

DON CLOTALDO *(To Rosaura)*: What have you done? This sacred place is prohibited to all by order of the king! *(To the Guards)* Arrest him!

SEGISMUNDO: Don't hurt him! I swear to God I'd rather tear out my own eyes than watch my friend suffer.

DON CLOTALDO *(To Segismundo)*: Arrogant Segismundo, your miseries are so great, by God's orders you died before you were ever born. You died in the paralyzed womb of your non-mother! You're a ghost, Segismundo, a flicker of reflected candle light—and you must remain silent and invisible. *(To the Guards)* Take the nonentity away!

(The Guards grab Segismundo. He resists. They disarm and beat him.)

ROSAURA *(Retrieving her sword)*: Don't hurt him!

SEGISMUNDO: Throw me in your deepest pit and I will rise up against you! I'll fly as high as I must! I'll enter Heaven itself to cut your throat—

DON CLOTALDO: Perhaps that's why you're imprisoned—to keep you from spoiling the Kingdom of God.

*(The Guards drag Segismundo offstage.
Clarín, found by a third Guard, is pushed into view.)*

ROSAURA *(To Don Clotaldo)*: Seeing how much arrogance offends you, sir, I'd be wrong not to humbly beg for my life. Please be moved by pity for me and my companion . . .

CLARÍN *(To Rosaura)*: If neither pride nor humility move him, well, maybe we could split the difference here?

DON CLOTALDO *(To Guard)*: Take their weapons and cover their eyes.

ROSAURA *(Before anyone can touch her sword)*: No! This sword once belonged to a nobleman. I can yield it to no one, sir, but you. No one below your rank may touch it.

CLARÍN: My sword, on the other hand, can be manhandled by any Spanish son of a bitch you can find. *(To Guard)* You, for instance.

(Clarín offers his sword to the Guard. Insulted, the Guard slaps Clarín across the face. Rosaura jumps the Guard, but is restrained by Don Clotaldo. The Guard drags the stunned Clarín away.)

ROSAURA: He's a poor old man! What kind of dishonorable nation insults and injures a harmless old clown?

DON CLOTALDO: Your sword, sir.

ROSAURA *(Swallowing her rage)*: If we're going to die . . . let us die with honor. I give you my sword as a testament to your—potential—mercy. It's a weapon of uncountable worth and must be respected—even if my life is not.

(Rosaura hands Don Clotaldo the ornate sword. He stares at it in disbelief.)

DON CLOTALDO: What is happening to me? Have I fallen asleep? Am I dreaming?

ROSAURA: That sword has a great secret and a great power; it's drawn me to Spain to avenge a wrong done to me . . .

DON CLOTALDO: Who gave this to you?

ROSAURA: A woman I knew.

DON CLOTALDO: What's her name?

ROSAURA: That's a secret.

DON CLOTALDO: More secrets! And how do you know this sword has secrets, too? And powers?

ROSAURA: The woman who gave me this sword said to me, "Go to Spain and find some way, through your natural genius, to make this sword known to the nobility there. I know, once this sword is seen, that one of the noblemen will favor you—and claim you as his heir."

DON CLOTALDO: . . . Which man?

ROSAURA: Full of superstitions and afraid he had died, she wouldn't repeat his name.

(Don Clotaldo walks away, examining the sword in his trembling hands.)

DON CLOTALDO *(To Rosaura)*: Twenty-five years ago the king decreed that anyone caught trespassing on this unlucky mountain must be put to death. Even if . . . my own dear son . . . were to break this law . . . and die as a consequence of my actions—my loyalty is to my king. I am his *valido* and my duty to him beats louder than my heart.

ROSAURA: Sir, you look at me with such sorrow . . .

DON CLOTALDO: It's as if my heart, sensing the presence of a kindred spirit, has run up to my eyes to see you, forcing my tears.

(Guards enter.)

ROSAURA *(Not understanding)*: Sir?

DON CLOTALDO: I don't know which of us has the greater trouble, my friend. *(To the Guards)* Bind him.

(The Guards hold Rosaura. Blackout.)

SCENE 3

Basilio's palace.
Duke Astolfo and Princess Estrella enter from opposite sides.

ASTOLFO: Goddess of starlight! Aurora borealis! Solar flare! Daughter of Apollo! Of rainbows! My soul, my happiness, my love, my war, my light! I could go on. Your voice is a flute! Your heart, a timpani! Your blood vessels are little pipes. Your corpuscles, little notes . . . to disembowel you would be to write a symphony in blood! One more time. A metaphor will do. Flowers are dishrags compared to you! Antelopes? Clumsy inedible venison compared to you. Helen? A slutbox. Aphrodite? Maggot poop. In short, you, princess, are stronger than the musk oxen, wiser than the Joshua tree, more industrious than the ants of the Amazon. Let me try that again. You are more poignant than the cross on which our savior suffered and died, more pointed than the thorns which pricked the divine brain, more forceful than the nails uniting God and humanity in a Crucifix of Understanding, and more delicious than the ultimate reunion He enjoyed with His Father—

ESTRELLA: Thanks, thanks, I think I get it.

ASTOLFO: But I haven't gotten a chance to praise each of your breasts—individually.

ESTRELLA: Cool off, duke. It's bullshit. Your words are flattering but they contradict your actions. Everywhere I look I see the machinery of war and the naked exercise of power politics. Pure destruction is your aim, Astolfo, not love.

(She starts to leave.)

ASTOLFO: Hear me out, *senorita*. Eugtorgius III was King of Castile. Basilio was his son. Basilio had two sisters. One was your mother, dear cousin, one was mine. Both grand dames are dead. Okay. Here it gets baroque. Basilio is old and feeble. He's inexplicably remote. Spends his days with mystics and clairvoyants and his nights watching cloak-and-dagger mysteries or hyperbolic *zarzuelas* or gazing at indecipherable modern paintings. His mind is nearly shot through with illusions and hobgoblins that could easily ruin the kingdom—and we all know his *valido*, Don Clotaldo, runs this country, *not* the king, and that must stop. Basilio's wife died twenty-five years ago in childbirth. That child is dead. Being more in love with astrology than sex, Basilio never remarried. His only heirs, unfortunately, are you and I. Your claim rests on the fact that your mother was the older of the two sisters and that you actually live in Spain. My claim, alas, the superior claim . . .

ESTRELLA: . . . rests on the accidental fact that you were born with a penis.

ASTOLFO: Perhaps in some future, distant century—the postmodern eighteenth or nineteenth centuries—a penis will mean exactly zero. But this is today, my dear, and we have to be realistic.

ESTRELLA: Get to the point.

ASTOLFO: Our declining uncle-king said he'd judge which of us is the proper heir to the Spanish throne. That's why I've left my native home in Poland to come here today. But it's not to make war, as you think—it's to offer a compromise.

ESTRELLA: I'm waiting for it.

ASTOLFO: My dear virgin princess, do you believe in love at first sight? Do you believe the gods of love are greater than the gods of war? Each of your breasts is a New World, Estrella—a world more fecund, more laden with gold and glory than the endless New Worlds discovered by your sailors. *(Estrella goes to speak)* Let me finish. My compromise is this: let's preempt our doddering uncle by getting married. Let's surrender totally to the gods of love. I'll be crowned king. You'll be my proud queen. We'll seal our claim to the throne in the damp, sticky bed of state—and rule Castile and the New World as one heart, one soul, one body.

ESTRELLA: Language has a strong effect on virgins. Your language is quite potent. I want the crown, Astolfo . . . and since I can't grow a penis to get the crown, perhaps I'll use yours instead. So if wanting you will get me some power . . . I might be talked into it . . . yes, I can feel myself beginning to want you . . .

(They get closer and closer. They nearly embrace—then she pulls back.)

. . . though I have to say your eloquence on behalf of love is contradicted by the sexy girl's picture you wear around your neck! Animal!

ASTOLFO: I can explain that—

(King Basilio, now mid-sixties, enters. Estrella and Astolfo go to him.)

ESTRELLA: Wiser than Jesus!
ASTOLFO: Nicer than Socrates!
ESTRELLA: Nicer than Jesus!
ASTOLFO: Wiser than Socrates!
ESTRELLA: We kiss your feet!
ASTOLFO: We lick the ends of your toes!

(They attempt to do these things, but Basilio stops them.)

BASILIO: I am moved by your sincerity, children. Come, niece, nephew, embrace the old body. Estrella, a little closer please. A little tighter. Just a bit more. You both love me! That's so nice. You should love me. I'm a great king and I have a great kingdom to give away!

ESTRELLA: Wiser than Jesus!

ASTOLFO: Nicer than Socrates!

BASILIO: But first I have something very important to tell you both. It weighs on me. Oppresses me greatly. Silence is all I ask of you at this moment of truth. You know I am called Basilio the Learned. I am called Basilio the Great. I am referred to in the epic poetry of Castile as Basilio the Beautiful. I like that last one very much. It's true, I run an empire in decline. A New World was given to us by God and we've depopulated it completely, pulled the last golden turds from its exhausted asshole—and have nothing to show for it but syphilis, the Reformation, and the disdain of history. Yes! The precious metals of America have destroyed this country as sure as any poison, because we weren't ready—we weren't ready! And now the French are at our doorstep! And what have we learned in our modern age, this Age of Anxiety? That the earth is no longer the center of the universe, and the human heart is nothing but a muscle. Still, we must go on! Anyway, you know I love mathematics. You know I'm a numerologist and can, by studying numbers in various relationships, tell the future. Basilio the Man Able to See the Future through Mathematics, I believe, is what they call me. You know I study the stars. You know the stars have many names: angels' tears, the perspiration of God, piercing rays of divine love, ancient pearls, light-infused originators of dreams, wish fulfillers, tablets of mystery, dandruff of Zeus, secrets of the universe written in nightly braille, the pressure points of Heaven, skyfire. They have been the object of my obsessive study and contemplation because they are the secret pages upon which God Himself types our future. A future very few—a gifted few, the geniuses of our time—are able to read. Children, I am such a man. Thank you, thank you.

(Beat.)

Twenty-five years ago my wife died giving birth to a freak. I told the kingdom its prince had died. It's a lie. I built a secret tower in the mountains, on the outskirts of the kingdom, among distant cliffs and sterile boulders where all-seeing sunlight never reaches. I published strict laws declaring nobody may enter the forbidden zone around those hills. In that tower, my unhappy son, this human viper, destroyer of my hopes and dreams, lives to this day.

(The voices of the Servant and Don Clotaldo, from Basilio's past, are heard.)

SERVANT'S VOICE: The boy burst through her body like a man-eating tiger . . .

DON CLOTALDO'S VOICE: He has your eyes, sire.

BASILIO: Untrustworthy doctors and astrologers who witnessed the birth of Segismundo were killed on my orders. Don Clotaldo himself killed them. Further, my *valido's* been the child's secret guardian, teaching this newborn tiger language, bringing him the civilizing word of God and the humanizing precepts of the one true Catholic Church. Throughout my reign, there have been rumors of a secret prince. My enemies, at home and in France, have searched the countryside for him. Sightings of false Segismundos have occurred all over Castile. Rumors and rumblings keep me up at night and frighten me. In my dreams I see a little boy chained to the rocks, crying for his father.

(Beat.)

I have three thoughts today. First, I love Spain, my Spain, very much. It was to spare Castile the rule of tyranny that I secluded my deformed child. Second, I have denied the prince his freedom and his rights. And that denial does not agree with Christ's teaching which says that in order to prevent tyranny I need not act like a tyrant myself. Third, it's possible I've made a serious mistake. What if all those prophecies, astrologers, all that number crunching, those eclipses and omens were wrong? It's possible he's inclined to tyranny and harsh violence—but it's an inclination eas-ily civilized by reason, kindness and prayer. For we all know the stars only point the way to the future—they don't create it. That task can only be fulfilled by One: by a God who's ordered that man's will be free, free to choose good over evil, free to think free thoughts. Here's my thinking. It will stun you. You think one of you will become supreme leader of Spain. Sorry—tomorrow I will place my son Segismundo on my throne instead. Without telling him he's my son, he'll be dragged out of prison, and placed on one of the most powerful thrones the earth has ever known. He'll have absolute power to govern and command you. Three things may happen. First, he'll be kind, intelligent and will disprove the prophecies of the neurotic stars. If that's so, you'll enjoy his enlightened rein. Second, he'll be cruel, monstrous and proud. He'll be the one-man holocaust the bloody eclipse predicted twenty-five years ago. If that happens, I'll re-imprison him instantly. Then, third, I will abdicate the throne, order a royal wedding, and make way for you two, Astolfo and Estrella, radiant king and queen of the Spanish State.

ASTOLFO *(Stunned)*: Is that what you really want?

BASILIO: It is my will. Do you question it?

ASTOLFO: If that's your will, let cousin Segismundo appear!

ESTRELLA: Let's meet this sudden and lucky new king!

BASILIO: Go to your rooms. It'll take a while to release my son from his chains, dress him, and make him ready. Tomorrow! Tomorrow you'll visit with the king!

ASTOLFO: Long live great King Basilio!

ESTRELLA: Long life—and sanity—to the king!

(Astolfo and Estrella kiss the King's hand and exit. Don Clotaldo, Rosaura and Clarín enter.)

DON CLOTALDO: A moment, dear sovereign?

BASILIO: A moment for you, old friend? A lifetime!

DON CLOTALDO *(On the verge of crying)*: Countless times I've come to you full of joy—and today, of all days, could've been my happiest.

BASILIO: Why is it we old men are always on the verge of crying?

DON CLOTALDO *(Sotto voce to Basilio, indicating Rosaura)*: That handsome boy has entered the forbidden tower and he's seen Segismundo. I know that means certain death. But he showed me an ancient sword which I had given to my dear Violante before I left her and broke her heart—I have an overwhelming feeling this boy is my . . .

BASILIO *(Laughs)*: You're a lucky man! If this crime had occurred twenty-four hours ago it would have meant the death of these prisoners. But today the sad story of my secret son has been told. It doesn't matter who knows it now. See me later. There's much I must tell you. There's much you must do for me. You'll be my right-hand man in the most amazing act of government the world has ever seen. These men you bring before me? Pardoned unconditionally.

DON CLOTALDO: May they praise your merciful name for a thousand years!

(Basilio exits.
Don Clotaldo goes to Rosaura and Clarín.)

Friends, you are free.

(Rosaura kneels at Don Clotaldo's feet.)

ROSAURA: I kiss these feet a thousand times! I mean that sincerely.

(Clarín doesn't move.)

Clarín?
CLARÍN: I'm still deciding.
ROSAURA: Get down and start kissing, fool!

(Clarín kisses Don Clotaldo's feet.)

You've given me a new life, sir. Please give your lifelong slave his first command.
DON CLOTALDO: I haven't given you a life. Any young man of breeding, once he's been offended as you have, has stopped living. You have no life until you've regained your honor—which can be done—honor, though fragile as a final breath, can be cleaned spotless, but it's something only you can do.
ROSAURA: What I must do to resurrect my fortunes is find swift, fierce and, if necessary, deadly revenge. Once my honor is cleaned in the blood of my enemy, my life will return to its former glory.
DON CLOTALDO: Take your sword. A sword that was once mine—I mean, mine while I had it in my hands today— knows how to avenge a wrong.

(Rosaura gratefully takes the sword.)

Your enemy, is he a great man?

ROSAURA: He's so great, in fact, I can't repeat his name.

DON CLOTALDO: But if you tell me his name you'll inspire me to fight with you.

ROSAURA: As I don't want you to think I undervalue your courageous offer to fight with me, I'll tell you. The man who wronged me—correction, ruined me—is no less than the great Astolfo, Duke of Warsaw.

DON CLOTALDO *(Taken aback)*: Astolfo.

ROSAURA: May the faithless hog be butchered and roasted a thousand times a day! I mean that literally!

DON CLOTALDO: But, my young lord, if you're Polish, then the good Duke of Warsaw is your lord, and a lord can never offend a fellow noblemen—

ROSAURA: Although he is my peer, he has disgraced me.

DON CLOTALDO: But he wouldn't dare slap a nobleman's face—

ROSAURA: His offense to me, sir, was far greater than a slap to the face . . . if you understand me.

DON CLOTALDO: I do not.

ROSAURA: I don't know what force of gravity draws me to you. Or why I feel an instant melancholy, an organic sympathy, when I look in your eyes, a sadness strangely mitigated by profound respect. This force forces me to speak. Look in my eyes, sir. Run your hand along the soft curves of my face. Listen to the strange pitch of my voice. Though I possess the swords and daggers of a man . . . I lack his "ultimate weapon."

CLARÍN *(Grabbing his own crotch)*: Get it?

DON CLOTALDO *(Getting it)*: ¡Ay cielos!

ROSAURA: Isn't it the ultimate insult for Astolfo to come to Spain to marry Estrella though he's had relations with me?

He's dirtied me, sir. He's disqualified me from the clean, legitimate bed of every nobleman in Europe. I've said too much!

(On the verge of tears, Rosaura exits. Blackout.)

SCENE 4

Hours later. The tower. Segismundo stares out a small window, crying.
  Don Clotaldo, wearing his mask, enters with food, drink and books.

SEGISMUNDO *(Wiping his eyes)*: Is there anything greater than freedom? If there is something—is it honor? If I had my honor would I be able to endure this?
DON CLOTALDO: I won't leave until I see you eat and drink.
SEGISMUNDO: What is honor? How do I know I have it?
DON CLOTALDO: Honor is . . . like that eagle you see flying out there. A king among birds, it disdains gravity and flies from the earth to the Heavenly ether like a quick fire, like lightning escaping the hollow clouds, like an ascending rocket.
SEGISMUNDO: I understand it now. Honor is a metaphor.
DON CLOTALDO: Drink.

(Don Clotaldo offers the drink.
  Segismundo drinks. The drugged drink effects him quickly. The lights begin to fade on him the sleepier he gets.)

SEGISMUNDO: What is honor to a prisoner? Master, there is greatness in me! Armadas and armies in me! I am a prisoner only by force. If I had my freedom, I'd bow to no man . . . I'd bow to no man . . . I'd bow to no man . . .

(Segismundo passes out.
Masked Guards enter.)

DON CLOTALDO *(To Segismundo)*: It's going to be a dark night, my prince. And all I see in this terrible darkness are clouds, eclipses and amnesia—it's like a calming killing gas is blanketing the sky . . .

(The Guards unchain Segismundo and lift him onto their shoulders. Blackout.)

⇜ ACT TWO ⇝

SCENE 1

The next day. The palace. Don Clotaldo and Basilio.

DON CLOTALDO: Segismundo's in your bed, sire: lethargic, oblivious. The machinery of state is poised to honor and serve him as if he were Your Majesty. Will you now tell me your purpose in this?

BASILIO: Can my experiment change Fate? Can it challenge the stars? Can I, a free man, made in God's image, can I alter my son's destiny and prove the astral prophecies of two decades ago false? Today Segismundo will learn he is my son, heir to the Spanish throne. He'll learn the extent of his absolute and riveting power. Then we'll see. He'll show us by his actions what he's been dreaming of doing all these years. If he's an enlightened despot he'll be allowed to remain. If he's a tyrant, he'll be sent back to his chains and his solitude.

DON CLOTALDO: Why did you command that I drug him? Why bring him to the palace asleep?

BASILIO: If he fails this test and must be forced back to that miserable life, knowing he's the real king, he'll surely lose his mind. But he fell asleep in his cell before coming here. And he'll reawaken in his cell again if necessary. Thus we'll be able to tell him he only *dreamed* he was king. And he'll accept that, knowing, as we all do, that all who live are dreamers.

DON CLOTALDO: I don't know if you'll succeed in this, sire, but it's too late now. He's been awakened and may be approaching.

BASILIO: I must withdraw. Speak to him, gentle friend, teach him as you have all his life. Be the golden thread that guides my son through his personal labyrinth.

DON CLOTALDO: Do I have permission to tell him it was you who ordered him imprisoned at birth?

BASILIO: If he knows everything, he'll understand all the dangers involved in this experiment, and he'll succeed.

*(Basilio exits.
Clarín enters.)*

DON CLOTALDO: Where's your master—your mistress? What's she—he doing?

CLARÍN: She's taken your advice, now she's a she again. And she's dressing the part. Rosaura's decided, since she's come out of the closet, to raid that closet for the finest girl's clothes in the kingdom.

DON CLOTALDO: That's proper and good.

CLARÍN: She's changed her name. And she's told everyone she's your niece. And that little white lie has sent her stock through the roof. She's now an honored lady-in-waiting to the nubile, eye-pleasing, come-hither-but-don't-touch-me-I'm-a-virgin Estrella.

DON CLOTALDO: That's good. As her uncle I can legitimately be responsible for her honor; she'll derive her honor strictly from me.

CLARÍN: Yeah, that too. About that other thing. The revenge-on-the-duke-thing. She says she agrees with you and she's going to bide her time and wait for the perfect moment.

DON CLOTALDO: Simply waiting is the best thing she can do.

CLARÍN: As for *me*—well, the world seems to have forgotten me: faithful Clarín who's tagged behind that stark, ungovernable girl for less than minimum wage for too long! But I tell you, sir, if I don't get something to *eat*, and *soon*, I'm going to sing like a friggin' canary and expose the whole lot of you double-dealers and flakes to every hack poet who'll listen!

DON CLOTALDO: Be my slave and you will eat every day.

CLARÍN: Not perfect. The slave part is not perfect. But okay.

(Music plays. Segismundo enters, accompanied by the Servant carrying a full-length mirror.

Segismundo, wearing the radiant clothing of a prince, head to toe in gold and jewels, gazes at himself in wonder as the Servant places the mirror on the ground.)

SEGISMUNDO: *Ay Dios*, what am I seeing? *Ay Dios*, what do I feel? What's this dreadful beauty? Why do I doubt it and believe it? God of Love, is this your son Segismundo? Is this me wearing silk and golden studs—and shoes? Is this me surrounded by lucid and spirited servants? Is this me among so many people dying to dress me and address me as "Your Lordship"? They say dreams are wonders. Wonders enchant and deceive. But I know I'm awake! I know, somehow, I am now splendid Segismundo! God, I didn't know what it was like to walk without chains! My God, please, if this is your promise of the future, keep it! Don't take it from me!

(Don Clotaldo approaches Segismundo.)

DON CLOTALDO: Give me your hand and let me kiss it. I am honored to be the first among the nobles of Castile to pledge you unconditional loyalty.

SEGISMUNDO: Your voice. You're Don Clotaldo. How is it possible? How can the man who mistreated me in prison be here, pledging his allegiance to me?

DON CLOTALDO: In the great confusion your new state creates in you, you experience a thousand natural doubts. But I wish to free you from that, if I may. You are, sir, the king's son, the prince, and the principle heir to the Spanish throne. You were secluded at birth and hidden in a desert tower because astrologers looking into your future predicted a thousand tragedies if you were ever to wear the crown. But trusting that your strength of character could vanquish the prophecies of the stars—because a magnificent soul can conquer anything—you've been brought to the king's palace from the tower in which you languished. This was done while you slept, while your soul was resting and peaceful. Your father will come to see you and from the king, Segismundo, you'll learn the rest.

SEGISMUNDO: Lawless traitor! Hypocrite! Subversive! What else do I need to know now that I know who I really am? You—Don Clotaldo—you have betrayed your nation by concealing me!

DON CLOTALDO: *¡Ay de mi triste!*

SEGISMUNDO: You've degraded the royal family and rebelled against the law! You've been unnatural and cruel to me! Now, as king, as law, and as myself—I condemn you to die by these hands!

(The Servant gets between Don Clotaldo and Segismundo.)

SERVANT: Your Majesty!

SEGISMUNDO: No one will hinder me!

SERVANT *(To Don Clotaldo)*: You must go!

DON CLOTALDO *(To Segismundo)*: I feel sorry for you, my son. You have the chance to prove yourself. But if you're barbaric and fierce, everything you see and feel will disappear.

(Don Clotaldo exits.)

SERVANT *(To Segismundo)*: Sir, I must say something . . .

SEGISMUNDO: I'm pleading with you to shut your mouth!

SERVANT: By keeping you in the tower the grandee was only obeying the law of the king!

SEGISMUNDO: If the king's law stinks it should not be obeyed!

SERVANT: Don Clotaldo didn't question the law or his king—

SEGISMUNDO: I predict a really hard time for anyone—*anyone*—who contradicts me today—

CLARÍN *(To Servant)*: Listen to your prince, fool!

SEGISMUNDO *(To Clarín)*: And who the hell are you?

CLARÍN: Oh, just an old clown with a big mouth; a fly, really, a dust particle . . .

SEGISMUNDO: Well, you're the only thing in this dreamlike world that makes me one bit happy.

CLARÍN: Can you translate that sentiment into food?

(Astolfo enters.)

ASTOLFO: May you achieve a kind of orgasmic happiness a thousand times a day, oh prince! Soul of Spain! Subduer of the Maya! Tamer of the Taino! Sovereign of the Old World, the New World and the Next World! You have emerged from the hot belly of those mountains like Christ clawing his way up from hell—a human sunrise, a resurrected hope, a Spanish Orpheus.

SEGISMUNDO: May God help you.

ASTOLFO: Uh-huh. Obviously you don't know who I am. That's the only excuse you have for not honoring me with

JOSÉ RIVERA

a little more passion and a lot more language. Here's a hint. I am Astolfo, Duke of Warsaw. Your cousin? We're equals?

SEGISMUNDO: If I say, "May God bless you," haven't I honored you enough? Watch yourself or next time I'll greet you with, "God save me from this fucking idiot!"

(Estrella enters. She's written her little speech on a piece of paper.)

ESTRELLA *(Reads)*: Majestic Father of the Spanish Civilization. You are most welcome to this throne which gratefully receives the round warmth of your royal rump and breathlessly desires union with you. Despite all the prophecies, which ranked you somewhat lower than Caligula, we know you will be a potent, plentiful and penetrating prince. Curtsy.

(Estrella curtsies. Segismundo gets closer to Estrella.)

SEGISMUNDO *(To Estrella)*: Who are you, princess? Who is this fallen angel—wingless—almost human; one part dirt, one part blood, one part starlight?

CLARÍN: *Cousin*, sire, the girl's your *cousin* . . .

ESTRELLA: Estrella is my name . . .

CLARÍN: . . . ambition is my game.

SEGISMUNDO: Many good things have happened to me, lady. Blinders have been taken from my eyes. Fetters have been removed from my legs. I've climbed the long road from Hell to Heaven in a day! But nothing has been quite as glorious as this glorious moment with you.

ESTRELLA *(Getting closer to him)*: You have a way with words.

ASTOLFO *(To Servant)*: If he touches her hand, I'm lost!

(Segismundo roughly grabs Estrella's hand and kisses it violently.)

SERVANT *(To Segismundo)*: Sire, what you're doing violates every single convention . . .

SEGISMUNDO: Didn't I tell you to get out of my way?

SERVANT: But she's Astolfo's lady. You insult him by . . .

SEGISMUNDO: I am the law now. I am convention. There can be no insult if I do what makes me happy!

SERVANT: But you said yourself if the law stinks it shouldn't be obeyed—

SEGISMUNDO: Every word out of your mouth is treasonous! Can anyone tell me the punishment for treason?

SERVANT: You can't punish me! I've been in this house all my life! I watched you being born! I watched your mother die!

SEGISMUNDO: I "can't"? Did you say I "can't"?

(Segismundo grabs the Servant. He sticks his thumbs into the Servant's eyes until they bleed. Blinded, bleeding, screaming, the Servant staggers out of the room. Estrella, shocked, follows him. Astolfo stares at Segismundo whose hands are bloody.)

I think I can.

ASTOLFO *(Shaken)*: Your Majesty . . . There's a difference between men and animals . . . that difference is law . . . and law is the codification of self-mastery and self-restraint . . .

SEGISMUNDO: Shut up, Astolfo. You're a blowhard and a bore.

ASTOLFO: Sire—

SEGISMUNDO: Relax—you don't want to lose your head over this little matter, do you?

(Basilio enters.)

BASILIO: What's happened here?

SEGISMUNDO: Nothing's happened.

(Segismundo holds out his bloody hands.)

Here are his eyes.

CLARÍN *(To Segismundo)*: . . . Excuse me, but that's the, you know, king?

BASILIO *(Horrified)*: Is that what this experiment has cost me? Has your freedom been paid for by a pair of eyes?

SEGISMUNDO: Is it the national pastime in Spain to speak in rhetorical questions?

BASILIO: My son, my prince . . . I came here expecting, hoping, that your good behavior would finally silence the arrogant stars . . . instead I walk in on a house of broken hearts . . . the servant blinded . . . the blood on your indifferent hands still warm. With what love can I touch you, my son, knowing the pain those fingers have caused? I came here with my arms out, hoping to embrace you, to welcome you to the society of men, to give a father's love, and to energize our nation with a swift reunion . . . no, son . . . I am afraid to look at you.

SEGISMUNDO: I can live without your arms, your embraces and your fatherly love, father—I've lived without those things all my life. And I can live without the insipid rhetoric of love, father! I used to ask my mentor: "What does 'father' mean?" And he'd define it for me a hundred different ways. And I never got it, father! You've kept me from your side . . . I've been no more than an *animal* to you . . . you've treated me like a malformation . . . an embarrassment . . . a godless spirit deprived of teaching, laughter, the violent colors of nature, experience, time and destiny. In the dirty war you've waged against me, in my two decades as a political prisoner, you have desired nothing less than my total mutilation . . . what do I care, Father, that you won't touch me now?

BASILIO: In the name of the Lord Jesus Christ, I ask to never be reminded that I brought you into existence!

SEGISMUNDO: If you hadn't given me life, I wouldn't have been offended. But you did give me life, and you did take it away, so you have offended me—

BASILIO: I freed you from the tower!

SEGISMUNDO: So you demand my gratitude? For what? You're an old and dying tyrant. I suppose you have no other heirs—no, you're incapable of really giving life—without another heir, you turn to me, your secret shame. Well, as prince, all of this—the empire itself, and every human soul *in* it—is mine by *law*. I owe you nothing. In fact, you owe me for the stolen years of imprisonment and abuse. I should have you arrested for theft! (*Shouts offstage*) Don Clotaldo, arrest the king!

BASILIO: Barbarian! Atrocity! Pillager! Living outrage!

CLARÍN: Eye-gouger!

SEGISMUNDO: All my life I've tortured myself, asking God what crime I committed. Now I know—my only crime was being born your son.

BASILIO: The astrologers were right about you! Be careful, prince! You are the heir to this throne and the first citizen of this state, but you must be humble and docile! Otherwise, be warned . . . you may be sleeping right now . . . and what you think is real may not be . . . the power you enjoy may be nothing more substantial than the power of a dream . . .

(*Basilio and Astolfo exit.*)

SEGISMUNDO (*To Clarín*): The power of a dream! Is the old man crazy? Am I imagining all this? No. I touch things;

I feel them. I am who I am! He'll regret what he said, you'll see. I disbelieve what I was and believe what I am: heir to the crown, the wronged, much-deceived prince, back from political exile. If he kept me in darkness it was not because of my weakness but because I couldn't know who I was. But now I know exactly what I am, what I've turned into courtesy of my dear dad: a crossbreed, a mixed-blood, a hybrid, half man, half animal.

(Rosaura enters, dressed as a woman. She does not see Segismundo and Clarín.)

ROSAURA: Estrella? Lady? Are you here?
SEGISMUNDO *(Seeing her)*: My God, who is that?

(Segismundo stares at Rosaura. She practices fencing moves in preparation for killing Astolfo.)

CLARÍN: So . . . big guy . . . what do you like most about being rich and famous?
SEGISMUNDO: The women.
CLARÍN: No surprise there.
SEGISMUNDO: Nothing I've seen since my sudden awakening has filled me with more contradictory and untranslatable feelings. They look peaceful but they fill my inner heart with tempests and whirlwinds. They speak softly but their voices echo in my memory at such volume that my head would burst. I once read, in one of the many theological treatises I ate, that God gave his best gifts and focused His greatest creative energy on making Man. Man—with the strength of mountains, the depth of oceans, the brilliance of fire—is Earth itself in miniature. But I think it was Woman God really loved. Woman—with the mystery of clouds, the depth of outer space, and the strange fires of

the Milky Way—is Heaven itself in miniature. Truly, the Earth is to Heaven as Man is to Woman . . . especially if she's the woman I'm looking at right now.

(Rosaura sees Segismundo, gasps, and starts to leave.)

Stay, lady, stay!

ROSAURA: I can't—

SEGISMUNDO: Don't bring in the sunlight of your presence only to flee and leave me in the cold shadow of night.

ROSAURA: Sunlight? Shadow? I don't know these flowery words . . .

SEGISMUNDO *(Recognizing her face)*: I don't believe what I see . . .

ROSAURA *(Recognizing him)*: Neither do I, sire! Good-bye!

SEGISMUNDO: I've seen your face before, lady.

ROSAURA: No, I don't think that's possible. *(To Clarín) Is* it, you worthless peasant slave?

CLARÍN: Impossible! Sire, have you seen the beautiful girls who live in the west wing of the palace?

SEGISMUNDO *(To Rosaura)*: But I look at you as if I'm looking at my own redemption, my own *life.*

ROSAURA: I have a job to do, my prince—

SEGISMUNDO: Dear woman—the two most excellent words a man may use in a lifetime of speaking—dear woman, who are you? Without knowing anything about you, I know I love you. I know it because, somehow, we've met before— maybe in a dream, in one of my few dreams of happiness! Please don't leave without telling me your name.

ROSAURA *(Trying to remember it)*: It's . . .

CLARÍN AND ROSAURA: Agnes/Astrea.

ROSAURA: Astrea. And I belong to Princess Estrella. I am her servant, a low and minuscule working woman with a busy schedule . . .

(Rosaura tries to leave. Segismundo stops her.)

SEGISMUNDO: I just don't understand how you—the obviously superior light, the greater beauty—should serve and honor that fading ragwoman Estrella. You, the real woman, should be empress here, not that counterfeit, pretending transparent forgery of a woman.

(Segismundo touches her face. Rosaura is frozen.)

ROSAURA: Since I crave your respect, sire, please let silence be my eloquent reply.

(Rosaura pushes his hand away and starts to leave.)

SEGISMUNDO: But you don't have to leave me! You understand what I'm trying to tell you!

ROSAURA: I understand it too well!

SEGISMUNDO: Then understand that all this coyness does nothing but provoke my anger, lady!

ROSAURA: Even if fury overcomes you, it can't destroy the respect and honor convention demands you have for me.

SEGISMUNDO: Convention! I blinded a man today, a nice man, a family man, probably had a house full of grandkids—kids he'll never see again—just to prove that I could do it!

(Segismundo grabs Rosaura.)

ROSAURA *(To Clarín)*: Bring someone, fool!

CLARÍN *(Calling off)*: Help!

SEGISMUNDO: I did it with these fingers! Fingers more than capable of stealing your precious chastity!

CLARÍN: Help!

ROSAURA (*Struggling*): Now I understand why the horoscopes said you'd desolate this kingdom and bring disgrace to your family and misery to your people! But what can the world expect from you? You're not really a man, except in name. Without a soul, without a heart, without reason, a language of curses, an appetite for slaughter—you're more *animal* than man . . .

CLARÍN: Help!

SEGISMUNDO: I spoke to you kindly! I used civilized phrases! I expect kindness and civility in return! Insult me and I have no choice but to answer you with the ultimate insult . . .

CLARÍN: Help!

(*Segismundo begins tearing off Rosaura's clothes.*)

ROSAURA: God help me!

(*Don Clotaldo enters.*)

SEGISMUNDO: In this room, I am God and animal!

DON CLOTALDO: I must stop you, prince, even if it means my death!

(*Don Clotaldo grabs Rosaura from Segismundo. Rosaura runs to Clarín, who holds her.*)

SEGISMUNDO (*To Don Clotaldo*): This is the second time you've provoked me, you pathetic, weak, old man!

DON CLOTALDO: There is no unlimited power, even for a prince! You must control this passion! You must civilize your heart!

(*Segismundo draws his dagger. Don Clotaldo kneels at Segismundo's feet. He grabs Segismundo's hands.*)

Kneeling at your feet, I will save my life!

SEGISMUNDO: Take your hand away!

(Segismundo pulls away from Don Clotaldo. The two men fight.)

ROSAURA *(Calling off)*: Don Clotaldo's in danger! Please help!

(Segismundo knocks Don Clotaldo to the floor. Astolfo enters to help. Seeing him, Rosaura and Clarín go into hiding. Astolfo gets between Segismundo and Don Clotaldo.)

ASTOLFO: But what is this, my prince? Is this how a king's sword is stained—with the cold blood of an old man?
SEGISMUNDO: His blood for my honor!
ASTOLFO: There's no honor in fighting a weaker man.
SEGISMUNDO: Then let me fight a stronger, if a stronger one exists!

(Segismundo draws his sword.)

ASTOLFO: I may kill a member of the royal family in self-defense.

*(Astolfo draws his sword. They duel.
Basilio and Estrella enter.)*

BASILIO: A duel? In my presence? What's happening here?

(Astolfo sheaths his weapon.)

ASTOLFO: Nothing, sire. We may both sheath our swords without losing our honor now that we're in your presence.
SEGISMUNDO: Much, sir, even though you are present. I was about to slaughter that cringing old bastard . . .
BASILIO: With no respect for his old age?

DON CLOTALDO *(To Basilio)*: It's only me, Your Majesty; this conflict is of no importance . . .

SEGISMUNDO *(To Basilio)*: It's absurd to ask me to respect old age. It's even more absurd to ask me to respect you. Some day soon, as I walk to the throne room, I'll walk on a carpet made of your gray hair, old man. That's the only way to repay you for the way you raised me.

(Segismundo exits.)

BASILIO: Before you take that walk, you'll return to your sleep, child. There you'll know that every good thing that's happened today happened in your imagination.

(Basilio and Don Clotaldo exit.)

ASTOLFO: Isn't it interesting, dear Estrella, how the prophets of doom are never wrong? You'd be the world's greatest psychic if you always predicted the worst. Just look at Segismundo. The stars were completely right about him. And isn't it interesting how the opposite never seems to happen? Look at me, for instance. My stars have always been good. My horoscopes bristled with happy news: conquests, applause, good looks, huge capital gains—and love—most of all, love. So why is it, princess, that my stars were wrong while Segismundo's were right? Why is it that instead of the love promised to me by the zodiac all I've gotten lately is a cold shoulder and an empty bed?

ESTRELLA: Oh, give me a break. Ask the girl whose picture you wore around your neck so close to your fickle heart the day we met. Ask her to read your tea leaves, Astolfo. Ask her to do your tarot cards. She's your confidante, your better self, your oracle and your soulmate—not me.

(Rosaura waits for Astolfo's answer.)

ASTOLFO *(To Estrella):* I swear on my mother's eyes to exorcise that girl's devilish likeness from the sanctuary of my heart, dear princess.

(Rosaura attempts to lunge at Astolfo, to tear him apart with her bare hands, but Clarín restrains her.)

The space left behind by the flight of that black angel will be filled with your light and likeness. You are brighter than the sun. An eclipser of the Crab Nebula. I'll get the picture right now—I'll give it to you and you can destroy it.

(Astolfo exits.)

ESTRELLA: Astrea!

(Rosaura and Clarín emerge from hiding.)

ROSAURA: Your ladyship! Employer! Visionary! You, who outfox the foxes of Spain!

ESTRELLA: I like you. You're the only woman in this murky cesspool of a palace I can trust with a really delicate matter.

ROSAURA: Your lowly slave doesn't deserve such honor.

ESTRELLA: Probably not, but I don't have much choice. All the girls around here hate me. Here's the thing. My cousin Astolfo is a man—I mean, he's *quite* a man. He's rich, royal, handsome and I hear the guy's got it where it counts. I mean, you're a not-too-bad-looking young woman . . . for a specimen of your class, I mean . . . I don't have to tell you about . . . the daydreams of a virgin princess . . . blind sexual attraction . . . fantasies the likes of which you've never experienced before . . . cold showers in the middle of the night . . . having to replace the damp bed sheets every morning! He talks too much and his metaphors drive me a little crazy, but the duke does something really wacky to my personal chemistry. Okay, but there's a problem. Something is standing in our way. The faithless hog—can you believe this?—keeps a badly colorized picture of an ex-girlfriend on a little gold chain.

CLARÍN *(Sotto voce, to Rosaura)*: Who could that be?

ROSAURA *(Sotto voce, to Clarín)*: Me, *bruto!*

ESTRELLA: Being a princess, I can't stand even the smallest competition and I've told him to bring it to me. And he's so spastically in love with me, he agreed. But being a noblewoman, it would be socially embarrassing to take the picture from him. That's where you come in. I want you to let Astolfo give you the picture, which you'll give to me, which I'll destroy thoroughly, okay? If you understand what love and all its humiliations are about, Astrea, you'll understand why I ask this of you.

(Estrella exits.)

ROSAURA: Oh God, I wish I didn't understand! Clarín, I need your advice. You have to tell me what to do!

CLARÍN: Advice is my forte, madam.

ROSAURA: I mean, who can figure this out? Who's got enough brainpower to keep up with the endless supply of nagging misfortunes in this damn place?

CLARÍN: Prudent reflection often yields an abundance of—

ROSAURA: I mean, does good old God just sit up there all day long, casually choosing the people He's going to pour extra misery on? Did I win some kind of perverse celestial lottery? I mean, what's a girl to do faced with these choices?

CLARÍN: Cooler heads may sort out the complexities—

ROSAURA: Am I too ashamed to act? Why am I jealous of Estrella? What about the prince? Before he attacked me—what was I feeling for him?

CLARÍN: Um...

ROSAURA: It's like capital "M" Misfortune is a strange variation of the mythological Phoenix: it burns itself out ruining your life until you're both consumed in its fire, and out of your dead ashes it comes back to life, stronger, ready to do more damage, promote more carnage—an endless cycle of regurgitated despair!

CLARÍN: I'm drawing a complete blank.

ROSAURA: Come on, Clarín! If I tell everyone who I really am, then Don Clotaldo, who saved my life, and holds his honor around me like a shield, and has asked me to sit passively by and do nothing, may be offended. And we know how bad offense is around here. But. If I don't tell Astolfo who I really am, and he sees me, how am I supposed to fool him? I'll deny to his face that I'm Rosaura, but my soul will give me away through my eyes—dammit—if I could just poke them out! That's it, Clarín: honor depends on blindness! If I could just find a pin to plunge into my eyes...

(Rosaura searches her clothes for a pin.)

CLARÍN: Madam!

ROSAURA *(Looking at him)*: You're right, what's the point? Whatever I do is only going to make things worse. It's my fate, wise Clarín, thank you for making that clear to me. It's my atrocious horoscope. I should just surrender to it. Let it win. Let it take me. Let this tortured soap opera reach its bloody climax and be done.

*(Astolfo enters, holding Rosaura's picture.
Rosaura pushes Clarín away. Clarín hides and watches.)*

ASTOLFO *(Seeing Rosaura, amazed)*: I don't believe this.

ROSAURA: What's the matter? Something wrong with you?

ASTOLFO: That voice. That legendary face. Through the windows of those eyes, I see the soul of my dear love Rosaura.

ROSAURA: Me? Rosaura? Your eyes play tricks on you, sir. My name is Astrea.

ASTOLFO: Drop it Rosaura, it's pointless. The soul doesn't lie. Not to one as deeply in love as I am.

(Astolfo tries to kiss Rosaura. She pushes him away.)

ROSAURA: Sir, Estrella—a woman Aphrodite herself would be proud to imitate—ordered me to ask you to give me that picture you hold in your hand—

ASTOLFO: Try that again. This time tell your eyes to play along with you. Tell your voice to convince itself before it tries to convince me. Come on, Rosaura, once more from the top! "Sir, Estrella—a woman Aphrodite herself . . ."

ROSAURA *(Blushing with anger)*: ". . . would be proud to imitate—ordered me . . ."

ASTOLFO: Very well. If you want to play games, we'll play games. "Ass-trea," was it? Ass-trea, as Duke of Warsaw, I command you to trot your tight little *Ass*-trea over to the princess, immediately, and tell her I honor her so much, I refuse to send her a mere copy of the beautiful Rosaura. Instead I'm going to send her the original: you.

ROSAURA: Sir. Originals are worth more than copies, true. But when an honorable person goes off having promised to perform a deed and then returns without having accomplished that deed—even if she returns with something of greater worth—then that person is a liar and a promise breaker. And liars and promise breakers have a special place reserved for them in the *Inferno* of my heart. I promised to get that picture from you and I will get that picture from you right now!

ASTOLFO: No.

ROSAURA: Damn you! I spit in your father's sperm!

(Rosaura tries to grab the picture. She and Astolfo tussle.)

ASTOLFO: 'Tis a fiery little bitch!

ROSAURA: I'll kill us both before another woman—especially that simpleton—touches this picture of me!

ASTOLFO: I'm enjoying this tussle, Rosaura!

(Astolfo has Rosaura on her back. He lies on top of her. Estrella enters.)

ESTRELLA: Astolfo, Astrea—what's all this tussling?

ASTOLFO: Estrella's here!

ROSAURA: Aren't you brilliant? *(To Estrella)* Lady, my lady, my lady . . . I can explain this, just give me a moment to order my thoughts.

ASTOLFO *(Panicking)*: What are you going to say?

ROSAURA *(To Estrella)*: You ordered me to wait here for Astolfo and ask him for that picture. I was alone. And, being alone, you know, the mind wanders, daydreams assert themselves, and since we were talking of pictures, I remembered I had one of myself, here, hidden in my sleeve. Crazy with boredom I took it out to look at it and I dropped it.

ASTOLFO: She dropped it.

ROSAURA: Astolfo the Brilliant, as he's referred to by the epic poets of Warsaw, both of them, came along with the picture of that other girl, ready to surrender it to you via me, and he saw my picture on the floor. And he's so adamantly opposed to giving you the picture of his sexy ex-lover that he actually intends to give you my picture instead! Which I can't let him do. When he wouldn't give me my picture, we tussled briefly for it.

ASTOLFO: I didn't enjoy that part at all.

ROSAURA: The picture Ass-tolfo holds in his hand is mine. Look at it, whose face do you see?

ESTRELLA *(To Astolfo)*: Give me the picture.

ASTOLFO: Do I have to?

(Estrella grabs the picture from Astolfo and looks at it.)

ESTRELLA: She's a true beauty with a dangerous and fiery spirit—and your twin, Astrea. Take it and get out of here.

(Estrella gives Rosaura her picture.)

ROSAURA: Now ask him for the other one, miss.

(Rosaura exits.)

ESTRELLA: Give me the picture I requested. Though I'll never look at it or refer to it again, I don't want it in your hands. Since I disgraced myself by asking for it, it has to be destroyed.

ASTOLFO: I live to serve you, you know that—oh gorgeous one—but I can't, I can't, don't make me . . .

ESTRELLA: You're a lying heathen and a shitty boyfriend! I don't want you to give it to me! If I had it, it would only remind me how I begged you for it!

(Estrella exits.)

ASTOLFO *(To Estrella)*: Does that mean the engagement's off? *(To himself)* Rosaura, Rosaura—Rosaura!

(Blackout.)

SCENE 2

The tower.

Segismundo, wearing animal skins, asleep, is being chained to the walls by the masked Guards.

Don Clotaldo and Clarín watch. Don Clotaldo is holding his mask.

DON CLOTALDO *(To Segismundo)*: Here you'll stay. Your tragedy ends where it began.

CLARÍN *(To Segismundo)*: As soon as you awaken, young prince, you'll understand what you've lost. Good luck has painfully mutated into its opposite. Your glory was pretended, your life was a fool's shadow, and your new destiny is death.

DON CLOTALDO *(To the Guards, indicating Clarín)*: Lock him up.

(The Guards grab Clarín.)

CLARÍN: Me? What did I do?

DON CLOTALDO: State secrets, national security—you understand—can't be trusted to someone with a mouth like yours.

CLARÍN: Correct me if I'm wrong, but did I threaten to kill my father? Did I squeeze out the eyes of a poor servant? Jesus, am I awake or am I dreaming?

DON CLOTALDO: Your big mouth has ruined you—are you so surprised?

(The Guards take Clarín away. Basilio enters, disguised.)

BASILIO: Trusted friend.

DON CLOTALDO: Sire? Is that you?

BASILIO: Stupid curiosity of mine. I came to see what's become of my son.

DON CLOTALDO: Closer to the animals than to God, once again.

BASILIO: Demolished prince, forgive me. What can I do? The stars predicted your misconduct. I have no choice if I'm to save my country.

SEGISMUNDO *(Dreaming)*: Eagles! Violent, necessary birds! I'm with you now! I'm your prince. Prince of the Skies! Prince of Freedom!

(Segismundo begins to wake up.)

BASILIO *(Wiping tears from his eyes)*: I can't let the child see me. I'll hide.

(Basilio hides. Don Clotaldo puts on his mask. Segismundo wakes up.)

SEGISMUNDO: What am I doing here? Where's the palace? Where are the servants? Am I back in the tower? God of Love, what have I been dreaming?

DON CLOTALDO: Ah! You're finally awake.

SEGISMUNDO: Am I?

DON CLOTALDO: I was starting to think you were going to sleep all day. You fell asleep the moment you saw that eagle flying by.

SEGISMUNDO: But I think I must still be sleeping and dreaming. If I have been dreaming—what I dreamed seemed so true—it makes me doubt what I see right now. Is it possible that while I'm asleep, I dream that I'm awake? This tower, these chains—this must be the dream!

DON CLOTALDO: I don't understand you . . .

SEGISMUNDO: No—it wasn't a dream! I saw those things—I woke up and saw a bed of bright colors, like flowers. I woke up in a garden of pleasures. Dozens of servants and pretty ladies dressed me in jewels and called me prince. You, teacher—you said I was the heir to the Spanish throne!

DON CLOTALDO: What did I get for telling you the good news?

SEGISMUNDO: I tried to kill you—twice!

DON CLOTALDO (*Laughs*): Twice!

SEGISMUNDO: I learned I had always been prince. So I sought revenge on everyone responsible for my years in exile.

(*Beat.*)

Except for one. A woman I loved. Loving her must have really happened to me. Hers is the one memory I still have on my skin . . . not the eyes of the poor man I crippled. Why? Why did I have to dream those things?

(*Basilio leaves his hiding place and exits, wiping his eyes.*)

DON CLOTALDO: We were talking about eagles as you fell asleep. So you dreamed of power. Let me tell you something. Even in dreams you should honor those who gave you life and raised you. Even in dreams there is right and wrong and you must do what's right.

SEGISMUNDO: That's true. And since we're dreaming now—and anything is possible in a dream—let me bury my animal side, as well as my anger and ambition. In this enchanted world, this world of mirages, to simply live is to dream. And since life is a dream, I know we don't truly wake up until we die. The king dreams he's the king and he rules and governs without knowing that all the praises he receives on loan are written on the wind and are soon turned to ashes and death. Who'd *want* to be king knowing that when he dies he's going to wake up and be nothing? Rich men dream of money—but money brings more grief than pleasure. The poor man dreams of his endlessly shrinking stomach. The pretender, the anarchist, the child, the ancient scholar, the pious, the lonely—all of them are dreamers, and none of them understands the dream! I dream I'm sitting in this muck, a convict—but I dreamed earlier I was happy, alive, powerful. Which was real? What is life? A frenzy. What is living? An illusion, a shadow, a fiction. The greatest good is nothing but a weightless idea. To live is to sleep, to live is to dream, all who live are dreamers, all dreamers are the dreams of God. And what is God Himself, but the greatest dream of all?

(Blackout.)

⚞ ACT THREE ⚟

SCENE 1

The tower. The sun and moon are in the sky. Clarín is chained to the wall.

CLARÍN: *¡Ay misero de mi! ¡Ay infelice!*
VOICES *(From off)*: Shut up! Quit your whining! Shut your hole! I'll give you something to cry about!
CLARÍN: I can't shut up! My name means "trumpet"—and I've got to trumpet my woes all over Creation!
VOICE *(Off)*: At least they haven't started torturing you! Just wait 'till you see what they do to your balls!
CLARÍN: HELP MEEEEEE! I'm trapped in a haunted tower! Buried alive because I know too much! Starving. Lonely—except for the rats and roaches. All my prospects, my old age, my retirement—up in smoke. Poor, pathetic, incarcerated me! Sapped, sacked, stolen, swollen me! And I'm having some really bad dreams here. Nightmares huddle around my soft, old brain. Oh, the things I've seen in my sleep. Crucified virgins! Tortured martyrs! All night my dream-self looks upon blood and gore and all night

I faint and gag. Now that I'm awake, I faint from *hunger*, from *silence*. I've become the patron saint of voicelessness. The shadow God of oblivion and secrets.

(The sound of drums. Many voices are heard offstage.)

IST SOLDIER'S VOICE *(Off)*: This is the cell where they're keeping him! Smash this door!
CLARÍN: Oh good, more miseries!

(Sound of doors being burst open. Soldiers enter.)

IST SOLDIER: There he is!
CLARÍN: No he isn't! Please! Don't torture me! I know you Spanish excel at it! But I hate the smell of my flesh burning! And please don't hurt my testicles!

(The Soldiers bow to Clarín.)

IST SOLDIER: Prince of Spain!!
CLARÍN: Oh, great, they're drunk too!
IST SOLDIER: We will fight and die under the banner of a native-born Prince of Spain—but never under the colors of a foreigner! Men, kiss his feet.

(The Soldiers kiss Clarín's feet.)

CLARÍN: Stop, that's really disgusting.
SOLDIERS: Long live our glorious prince!
CLARÍN: So let me get this straight. It's actually a tradition in Spain to take wretched prisoners out of jail and make them Head of State?
IST SOLDIER: We've told your father the king that we'll recognize only you as our sovereign leader—not that foreign usurper Astolfo, Duke of Warsaw.

CLARÍN: My father's the king?

1ST SOLDIER *(To other Soldiers)*: He's delirious from the constant torture and bad food—and being in this tower has aged him badly. Real badly. Those criminals in Basilio's gang will pay for this, Your Lordship. Long live Prince Segismundo!

SOLDIERS: Long live Prince Segismundo!

(The Soldiers break Clarín's chains and set him free.)

CLARÍN: I get it now. Every guy you do this to is renamed Segismundo. Okay! I love that name!

(Segismundo enters, his arms and legs in chains.)

SEGISMUNDO: Who calls my name? Who calls Segismundo?

CLARÍN *(To Segismundo)*: Don't walk in here *now*, for Chrissakes!

1ST SOLDIER: Will the real Segismundo make yourself known to us?

SEGISMUNDO: I am Segismundo.

CLARÍN: *Ay Dios*, I'm screwed on so many levels—

1ST SOLDIER *(To Clarín)*: How dare you impersonate the Prince of Spain?

CLARÍN: Me? You're the one who re-baptized me Segismundo! You're the one who scribbled Segismundo on my birth certificate! You're the one—

1ST SOLDIER *(To Segismundo)*: Fair prince. Your father lied to you. You were not dreaming when you were in the palace. They drugged you and dragged you out of prison and put you on the throne. When they didn't like what happened they drugged you again and re-imprisoned you. Now the incogitant king and his senile staff wish to give our fair Castile to foreigners. To Polacks! But the people, hearing that a true native-born prince exists, have risen up against

your father. We've come in vast numbers, a true guerrilla
army of bandits and peasants, to give you freedom and
fight at your side.

VOICES *(Off):* Long live Prince Segismundo!

SEGISMUNDO: *¿Otra vez? ¿Que es esto, cielo?* God, am I dream-
ing again? Must I suffer this recurring dream until I die?
Am I to be overjoyed by the promise of great power—only
to lose it again? No, you can't make me hope again, only
to take it away. In a prison like this, in a life like this, hope
is too risky. I know life is a dream. I know you floating,
insubstantial men are the shades and handpuppets of an
evil Dreamer—a God determined to make me crazy. Yes,
I know you well! And I know myself. I'm a sleeping man
sick of pretended sovereignty and make-believe fame and
simulations and masks. I'm wise now and you can't
deceive me anymore.

1ST SOLDIER: If you think we're illusory, look out that win-
dow, gaze at the carpeted mountains, and see the popula-
tion of a great dominion assembled to honor you.

SEGISMUNDO: I've seen it before. I've dreamed it already.

1ST SOLDIER: Great events in history, my lord, are often fore-
told in dreams. The premonitions, déjà vu, and shadows of
the mind are often truer than reality. If you've already
dreamed all this, then your vision was a mere prologue to the
grandest turning point in our history. As I live and breathe,
good prince, this moment lives. Seize it now before it passes.

SEGISMUNDO: You speak well—that's a dangerous quality in
a man of action. Perhaps you're right. Perhaps my dream was
a pre-indication—an inspiration—to my waking self. And
if not—if our short life is but a dream—so be it. Let's dream
then. And let's be aware that our pleasure could all disap-
pear at a moment's notice. Let's remember that all is tem-
porary. All life is borrowed and must be returned. Know-
ing this, let's risk it all, my loyal soldiers, and not be afraid.

Let's dream of conquest and justice! Let's dream of armies
and liberation! Let's dream of honor and sweet revenge!
Let's show Basilio just how right his astrologers were!

SOLDIERS: *¡Viva Segismundo, viva!*

SEGISMUNDO: And death to foreigners!

SOLDIERS: Death to foreigners!

*(The Soldiers break Segismundo's chains and set him free.
Don Clotaldo enters, masked.)*

DON CLOTALDO: What is this? What's happening here?

CLARÍN *(To Don Clotaldo)*: You better cover those eyes, boss!

DON CLOTALDO *(Taking off his mask)*: Now that you're free
again, and powerful, surrounded by loyal soldiers . . . I know
you have to kill me for what I've done to you. All I ask is
you do it quickly and tell the world I did not beg for mercy.

(Don Clotaldo kneels.)

SEGISMUNDO: *Levanta, levanta, padre . . .*

(Segismundo helps Don Clotaldo to his feet.)

. . . my true father. You raised me, taught me, strengthened
me in a world that would have wasted me otherwise—let
me embrace you in gratitude.

(Segismundo embraces Don Clotaldo.)

DON CLOTALDO: What is this?

SEGISMUNDO: A dream, of course. But this is a dream I will
control. You said yourself, even in dreams we must do
what's right. So I will dream humility and generosity
toward those I owe my life to and destruction and hope-
lessness toward everyone else—my father most of all.

DON CLOTALDO: In the spirit of doing what's right—if that's your credo—you have to understand what I must do. I can't go against your father. I can't march in your army. Basilio is my king and my friend and like everyone in the kingdom—including you men—I owe him absolute and unconditional loyalty. If that makes me a threat, Segismundo, then do what you must to punish me.

SEGISMUNDO: You're an old idiot, Don Clotaldo, and a fool!

(Segismundo takes a Soldier's sword and raises it as if to strike Don Clotaldo.)

The nerves and demons in my body beg me to silence you . . . but I won't. No one deserves to die for being loyal. And just knowing this is a dream checks my passion and inhibits me. I know when I wake up again, I'll see you here, bringing me food and books . . .

DON CLOTALDO: My prince . . .

SEGISMUNDO: Go. Obey your loyalty. Do what common sense tells you. Don't stand here arguing with us—each man has his own definition of honor.

DON CLOTALDO: I must fight for the Spain of King Basilio.

SEGISMUNDO: Then I'll see you on the battlefield, my friend.

DON CLOTALDO: On the battlefield.

(Don Clotaldo and Segismundo embrace, kiss. Don Clotaldo exits.)

SEGISMUNDO *(Kneeling in prayer)*: Don't wake me up, dear God. Don't do it. If I'm awake, don't let me fall asleep. Whether we're shadows or not, it's important to do what's right and what's honorable. Let's go!

(Blackout.)

SCENE 2

The palace. The sun and moon are closer together. Basilio and Astolfo are suiting up for battle.

BASILIO: Who can stop the furious charge of a horse gone wild? That's what my people have become. Inflamed adolescents! Gangsters and sycophants. They disappoint me greatly! Half the country is screaming, "Long live Astolfo." The other half is crying, "Long live Segismundo." Rioting and destruction is all they know to give me, when they should be giving me loyalty, obedience and taxes. It's anarchy! We might as well be living in France!

ASTOLFO: Today was to be my coronation day: a day I've waited for all my life. I'm not going to let a mob of unclean paupers ruin it! They want tough? They want a little demonstration of ruthlessness? They want to see if I have the right stuff to be king? Somebody get my horse!

BASILIO *(Fighting tears)*: It's all my fault. This had all been predicted and I tried to sneak around the stars and they've come back to punish me. The more I tried to avoid it, the worse it became. I've destroyed my own kingdom, Astolfo.

ASTOLFO: When I'm king, things are going to be different around here, you can be sure of that. One Spain, completely united, utterly Catholic. The Earth will once again be the center of the universe!

(Basilio cries. Astolfo exits. Estrella enters.)

ESTRELLA: Cry. Fine. Good way to stop the bloodletting, uncle! Stop that! I've got such a headache. Today was supposed to be my wedding day. I was supposed to be crowned queen today. Instead I'm watching effigies of myself burning all over Madrid! Christ, do something! I'm seeing eyes being torn out of faces, common street corners turning into instant graves and the proliferation of orphans and ghosts. Every flower in the kingdom covers someone's tomb. Every citizen is an accomplice to murder. Those not killed in the fire of this civil war are choked by the smoke of unbearable sorrow . . .

BASILIO *(Controlling himself)*: Yes. And it must be brought to a sudden ending.

ESTRELLA: And another eclipse threatens to swallow the world.

BASILIO *(Calling out)*: My horse! I will slaughter my upstart son myself if that's what it takes to save the kingdom!

ESTRELLA: Please let me fight with you! I was born for combat!

BASILIO: Come, princess! Every soldier is welcome!

(Basilio and Estrella exit. Rosaura enters, pursued by Don Clotaldo.)

ROSAURA: Everything is war! War is everything!

DON CLOTALDO: What are you going to do?

ROSAURA: This war gives me the chance to do what I've waited much too long to do.

DON CLOTALDO: Kill the man destined to be the next King of Spain?

ROSAURA: I'm tired of waiting for you to do it for me, sir.

DON CLOTALDO: But Astolfo saved my life.

ROSAURA: And ruined mine.

DON CLOTALDO: Jealousy has ruined you.

ROSAURA: You don't know what jealousy is. Since seeing me, Astolfo has gone every night to Estrella's bed—she forces me to wait on her and I hear them on the other side of the door. That's right, the virgin princess is no longer!

DON CLOTALDO: My girl, you're lost. You're determined to die.

ROSAURA: So be it. My good name inspires me to this. My self-respect implores me. My anger justifies me. There's no other way, good sir, there's no other way!

(Rosaura exits. Blackout.)

SCENE 3

An open field. Upstage, a pile of rocks. The sun and moon are approaching total eclipse.

Segismundo is wearing animal skins. Soldiers and Clarín are at his side.

SEGISMUNDO: *¡Ay, si este dia me viera Roma!* Rome would see a resurrected barbarian lifting his sword to command the world's greatest army! Flattening the fortresses of Heaven would be too easy! But no, good soldiers. I should be careful. Such arrogant language could hurt me. If I awaken . . . and all of this has been an illusion . . .

CLARÍN: Look! A beautiful woman on a dappled horse! Or is that a dappled woman on a beautiful horse? Or a dappled horse on a beautiful woman? Or a . . . ?

SEGISMUNDO: She's brilliant, lucent . . .

CLARÍN: Hold on, it's Rosaura.

SEGISMUNDO: God's brought her back to me.

(Rosaura enters, dressed in the traditional skirts of a peasant woman, with her ornate sword.)

ROSAURA: Generous prince! You've been reincarnated from shadows and awakened to a new life, like a new sun rising over a glorious New World. Please let an unfortunate woman speak with you. Please let my status and my sex inspire your compassion and your chivalry.

(Beat.)

Three times this hybrid-woman—half-Spanish, half-Polish—has come to you in three incarnations. The first time, I was dressed as a man. I met you in the tower and you were an animal with a man's heart and your troubles made mine look small and I pitied you. The second time, you saw me as a woman, a low servant, and you were the most resplendent and horrifying of kings. Indeed, in that grim nightmare afternoon you were a man with an animal's heart: you blinded a man and you attacked me. This is the third meeting. And today I am both man and woman. I am dressed for war as a man. But beneath my armor is a woman's broken heart. Today I am myself.

(Beat.)

Sir, my father left Poland, and my noble mother Violante, years ago—leaving behind only his sparkling sword and her shattered hope. Like some kind of god he had descended on her, radiant with stolen gold, pompous and smooth and very Spanish. A few months later he dishonored her by leaving her—despite his many promises— naked, unwed, breathless and pregnant with me. I was the result of a young man's charming words and a young woman's willingness to believe. And if I haven't inherited my mother's beauty, I have inherited her luck: I too have been dishonored by a man. It was the Duke Astolfo of Warsaw. Just saying that faithless name—look at me!—is enough to inspire tears of hatred. Indeed, for a long time, after he loved me and left me to colonize his cousin, I went insane. I swore I heard my thoughts spoken aloud by village savants who had kidnapped my mind. I ate dirt. I cut my arms. I lay in bed counting spiders. I developed a hatred of even numbers. If I counted an even number of spiders, I'd eat one. I tried to kill myself several times. I lost the power to speak! It was my mother who brought me back from the dead. Breaking a twenty-five year silence, my mother told me her own pitiful, secret story. Hearing her confess her own folly put me outside myself. And that's when I decided to live—and to avenge her honor as well as my own—that's when I decided this cycle of rape and abandonment would end with me. Shielded with my mother's blessings and armed with my father's sword, I came to Spain and now I've come to you.

(Beat.)

You have a chance to avenge the wrongs done to you. You are justified in the eyes of God and man. I ask you to let me stand at your side, to fight at your side, and let me find my revenge. Let the field of combat be the site of my life's recovery. I've come here to serve you with my woman's spirit and my manly sword—yet—if you try to seduce me as a woman, I'll cut your throat as a man. If that's understood, generous Segismundo, let's proceed into battle and win this war of love.

SEGISMUNDO: How is it possible for you to know so much about my dream? All those things you mentioned: the blinding, the attack, were the violent shadows of my sleeping self . . . impossible for you to know—unless . . .

ROSAURA: It wasn't a dream. It was true. I was there.

CLARÍN: So was I. For most of it.

SEGISMUNDO *(To Rosaura)*: I'll help you restore your honor, by the God of Love, I will! Sound the alarms!

(Sound of trumpets. Segismundo addresses his Soldiers:)

Ultimately we can't know what's real and what isn't. How do we know that every past moment of happiness and glory wasn't dreamed? How do we know that all happiness will not end in disenchantment? How do we know that death isn't the final awakening? And when we finally awaken and look into the face of the Dreamer who made us all—what will we see there? Our questions are unanswerable. These ultimate truths—unknowable. All is confusion and chaos! In this anarchy of the mind, let's try to find some hope and happiness—and love. Let's do it before love turns to sorrow. Let's do it in the brief time we have on earth. Above all, let's gain something eternal—something that outlasts lifetimes and dreams. Let's try to win some glory and honor and let's hope they last a few good moments—if not forever.

ROSAURA: Segismundo! I'll fight with you!

SEGISMUNDO: Dear woman, I'll avenge your honor before I seize the crown.

(Trumpets. Segismundo and Soldiers exit. Before she can exit, Rosaura is stopped by Clarín.)

CLARÍN: Before you go, madam, I have to tell you what I've learned. I know who you are! I know Don Clotaldo is—

(Battle sounds: trumpets, cannons, shots, screams.)

ROSAURA: Segismundo's being attacked! He's surrounded! I can't be afraid, Clarín! I must be at his side!

(Rosaura exits.)

VOICES *(Off)*: Long live Astolfo!
VOICES *(Off)*: Long live Segismundo!

CLARÍN: Long live Astolfo *and* Segismundo! Long live everybody! Stop the fighting, you assholes! Ugh, look at yourselves. All that waste. Shame on all of you! You build a civilization—for that? To burn it to the ground? You raise a child in order to put a sword in his hand?

(A bullet whizzes over Clarín's head and he hits the ground.)

I better shut up and get my ass to some safe hiding place—away from all this unrestricted hooliganism and machismo! Some place where Death will never find me!

(Clarín crawls to the upstage rocks and hides behind them. Soldiers from both armies enter and fight, then exit. Basilio, Don Clotaldo, Astolfo and Estrella enter—all are bloody.)

BASILIO: Has there ever been an unhappier king? A more disrespected father?

DON CLOTALDO: Our forces are in full retreat . . .

ASTOLFO: The traitors are winning!

ESTRELLA: Loyalists and patriots are the ones who win wars—*we're* the traitors now, Astolfo . . .

BASILIO: We must escape to the New World before Segismundo finds me.

(Shots are fired. Clarín falls from behind the rocks. He staggers downstage, mortally wounded.)

CLARÍN: Fucking great! Oh, this is bloody brilliant!

ASTOLFO: Who is this clown?

CLARÍN: Oh, just some joker who thought he could run away from Death and ran smack into it. Oh, this hurts. This is mortal! Before I go—some advice. Next time you want to avoid dying in war, run straight into the middle of the battlefield. Don't go hiding behind tons of protective granite. 'Cause, I'll tell you, if God really wants your ass, He's going to get your ass . . .

(Clarín dies.)

ESTRELLA: "If God really wants your ass, He's going to get your ass."

DON CLOTALDO: What strange eloquence.

BASILIO: The clown's right. The more you run from Fate, the quicker it finds you. It's foolish to run from the decrees of God and the stars.

DON CLOTALDO: True, but a wise man must try. Stars may prove false. And God's will is often ambiguous and subject to interpretation. Let's run.

ASTOLFO: Don Clotaldo's right. We should run, my lord. He'll protect us as we go.

BASILIO: No. If God's verdict is "Death," then Death is what I'll face, here, in the heart of my country.

(Basilio, Don Clotaldo and Estrella exit. Rosaura enters, sees Astolfo and attacks him.)

ROSAURA: Rapist!

(Rosaura and Astolfo fight. Rosaura stabs Astolfo with her ornate sword. He falls, wounded. She stands over him, ready to strike again.

Estrella runs in. She moves to Astolfo and covers his body. She looks up at Rosaura, her angry eyes plead for mercy.)

ESTRELLA: Noooooooo!

(The sun and moon are in total eclipse.

Rosaura cuts off Astolfo's ear. When Rosaura sees Clarín, she lets out a cry, and prays over his body.)

Basilio and Don Clotaldo enter, chased by Segismundo's Soldiers. They surround Basilio. Segismundo enters, Basilio kneels before him.)

BASILIO: If you're looking for me, here, find me in the dirt, my son. Take my gray hairs and wipe your feet on them. Step on my back on your way to the throne. Take my disgraced crown, my broken reputation and my sullied honor, and destroy them all. Make a slave of your senile parent and you'll finally fulfill the promise of the stars.

SEGISMUNDO: Listen to me, all of you. Whatever God writes in the book of destiny is final. It can't be rewritten. It can only be misinterpreted. My father tried to save himself from the iron words of destiny and, in so doing, turned me into an animal, though it was possible—with a normal childhood, cherishing my natural gifts and sharpening my intelligence—I would have grown up to be a fair and tolerant monarch. We'll never know. By trying to keep me from being wild, he made me wild! If someone told you this sword would kill you, would you deliberately put it to your throat? Injustice and revenge will not help you overcome your fate—only reason, tolerance and tranquillity of spirit will. Let all of you who are watching this conquest remember it as the illustration of the astrologers' predictions: a kingdom left bleeding, a royal family compromised and a good king reduced to slavery. All of it has come to pass. How am I, who am younger, and spiritually weaker than this man, able to overcome the fate he could not?

(Beat.)

King Basilio, stand. Let me take your hand, dear father. Now that you're enlightened and know your errors—here

163

I am—I kneel before you and surrender myself and my treasonous armies to your authority. Take your revenge on us as you see fit.

(Basilio stands. Segismundo kneels at Basilio's feet.)

BASILIO: You're my son. Such incredible mercy and wisdom—you're my proper son—again! You've conquered this nation in legitimate battle—and pardoned me in a noble act of compassion—you've truly earned the right to be called King of Spain.

ALL: Long live King Segismundo!

SEGISMUNDO *(To Basilio)*: The legitimate battle I've fought today hasn't been on the naked earth or under the judgmental sky, but in my tumultuous spirit, where a war between a bestial nature and a human one has been waging since birth. I've won a great victory over myself today. *(To the others)* Don Clotaldo will be fully pardoned for all the years of my incarceration. Astolfo and Estrella will be restored to their proper places in the royal family. They will wed immediately.

ESTRELLA AND ASTOLFO: Thank you, my lord.

SEGISMUNDO: And Clarín—*Don* Clarín—will be buried with full military honors.

1ST SOLDIER: And the tower?

SEGISMUNDO: Level it. Erase it. Consign it to memory and never build another one.

(Estrella, Astolfo and Basilio exit. The Soldiers carry away Clarín.

Rosaura approaches Segismundo, as Don Clotaldo watches from a distance.)

ROSAURA: My king? What about me?

SEGISMUNDO: I have two regrets. I'm sorry I ever raised a hand against you in lustful anger; I'm sorry I tried to crush your spirit. If you can, please forgive me.

ROSAURA: You were insane then. Seeing how much you've changed, how wise and gentle you are, I can forgive you.

SEGISMUNDO: Dear woman—nearly sister and twin . . .

ROSAURA: Don't call me sister. A sister can't do this.

(Rosaura kisses Segismundo.)

SEGISMUNDO: My second regret, dear Rosaura, is this: now that I know I'm the king's son, I don't think I'm able to love you and wed you as I wish. Because you're not of noble birth, convention forbids . . .

DON CLOTALDO: Rosaura is a noblewoman, Your Majesty, as highly born as any in Europe. Rosaura, I'm the man who dishonored Violante, your mother—may she forgive me someday. I'm your father.

ROSAURA: I think I've always known it, sir.

(Rosaura returns Don Clotaldo's sword to him. They embrace. He exits.
Rosaura turns to Segismundo.)

SEGISMUNDO: What if . . . ? Rosaura, I'm afraid . . . what if I wake up too soon . . . and all this is once again a shadow's shadow and I'm alone, screaming in a prison cell . . .

ROSAURA: Don't say it. Don't question it. Just let it happen to you. If it's a dream, good. Perhaps I'll wake up myself. Perhaps I am the dreaming God that finally forgives you for being born. Perhaps all this is *my* dream, with you in it. I like that one! Either way we can let our dreams teach us about the brevity of life and the fleeting nature of happiness. If life *isn't* a dream . . . and I don't think it is . . . even better. We make it what we want. We stay and build on the past. Or we forego royalty and go to the New World on the next ship to start all over. If *la vida no es sueño* . . . that means this is it, my prince, my love. This is the only life there is.

(Segismundo and Rosaura kiss.
   The eclipse ends. Bright sunlight fills the stage.
   Blackout.)

END OF PLAY

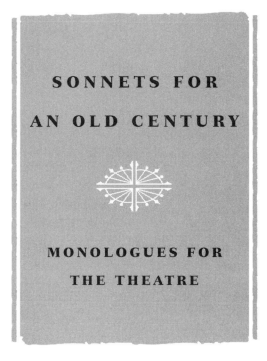

SONNETS FOR
AN OLD CENTURY

MONOLOGUES FOR
THE THEATRE

For my father,
Herminio Rivera

SPECIAL THANKS TO

Juliette Carillo, Olivia Honneger, John Ortiz, Michi Barall, Geno Silva, Yusef Bulos, Alene Dawson, Sam Wellington, John Socas, Laura Tishler, Damian Young, Yancy Arias, Marin Hinkle, Susan Knight, Jaime Sanchez, Irma St. Paul, Daphne Rubin-Vega, Kevin Carroll, Jojo Gonzales, Ching Valdez-Aran, Chris McCann, Jonathan Lisecki, Felicity Jones, Jessica Hecht, Jaye Austin-Williams, Missy Pyle, Gary Perez, Stephanie Berry, Rob Campbell, Larry Ash, Brian Dinges, Ben Hammer, Kathleen Wallace, Rachel Malkenhorst, Jesse Borrego, Richard Coca, Dawn Saito, Alex Fernandez, Tom Lenoci, Michael Manual, Marissa Chibas, Tony Abatemarco, John Vargas, Natalie Griffiths, Melody Butiu, Camilia Sanes, Moisés Kaufman, Kevin Jackson, Corey Madden, Lisa Peterson, Neel Keller, Elizabeth Bennett, Michael Greif, Christine Jones and Julia Edwards

Sonnets for an Old Century was developed by the Relentless Theatre Company, New York Theatre Workshop, The Mark Taper Forum, The Philadelphia Theatre Company, The La Jolla Playhouse, Ensemble Studio Theatre West and CalArts.

Sonnets for an Old Century received its world premiere production at the Greenway Arts Alliance (Pierson Blaetz and Whitney Weston, Co-Artistic Directors) in Los Angeles, California, on January 14, 2000. Oscar Arguello, Laura Frank and Maricela Ochoa were co-producers. It was directed and designed by James Eric; scenic art was by Gabriel Dell, Jr.; lighting design was by Cheryl Waters; costume design was by Naomi Yoshida-Rodriguez and the stage manager was Irma Escamilla. The cast was as follows:

Antoinette Abbamonte	Lesa Carlson
Andrew Carrillo	Gary Carter
Juan Carlos Cisneros	Lynn Dandridge
James DiStefano	Mark Ferreira
Valentina Ferreira	Gretchen German
Billy Kane	Newton Kaneshiro
Kevin Kelly	Wendy Johnson
Diana C. Larios	Javi Mulero
Masashi Odate	Rosana Potter
Reiko	René Rivera

Steven Ruge   Michael Teisan
Kiersten Van Horne   Whitney Weston

NOTE: For a while, the monologues had no character names—so I gave each monologue a name, the names of my favorite actors, as a kind of "payback" for all their years of support and free work. This is in no way meant to limit the type of actor best able to perform that monologue. Consider the names to be a flexible marker as to character identity. In many cases, gender, age and race are undetermined—in production, please aim for the maximum level of diversity.

(i who have died am alive again today,
and this is the sun's birthday; this is the birth
day of life and of love and wings: and of the gay
great happening illimitably earth)

—e.e. cummings
"I THANK YOU GOD"

The afterlife could be represented by a tunnel, a cave, a warehouse, an airplane hangar, catacombs or a seedy office building with ugly fluorescent lighting—but it's a large space.

The recently deceased people who appear in the space are from various parts of the U.S. There are Latinos, blacks, Asians, whites. There are gays and straights, children and old people. All are strangers to each other. Wendy Johnson speaks to them.

WENDY JOHNSON

You stand here and make your statement.

That's it.
You want to fight with existence?
Go for it. You want to scream?
Knock yourself out.

Just remember:
your words go out to the universe,
all your words, to be, I don't know,
recycled among the living—like
rain, like part of—
some ecology of the spirit.

It's the last and only time you have
to give your side of the story, as
far as I know.

JAVI MULERO

We would eat liverwurst on black bread
with mustard and onions and have sex.

We would have sex on tattered, sticky
pages of the Sunday *New York Times*.

We would have sex after walking
across the Brooklyn Bridge, cold
October afternoons, staying home from
work, angry at our office jobs among
the walking dead and art wanna-bees.

We would have sex instead of air.

We would have sex while burning
garbage fell on our fire escape
because the maniac on the floor above
us decided devils were living in his trash.

We would have sex while water dripped
through our ceiling because the
maniac on the floor above us kept the
water in his bathtub running while he
went off to visit a brother on Staten
Island who had communicated with
devils and had salient advice on how
to use them for your own benefit.

We would have sex while the maniac on
the floor above us returned from
Staten Island, fell in the hallway,
and pounded the floor with his fists.

We would have sex after visiting the
maniac on the floor above us, his
eyes black and blue, his shirt
saturated with blood, who told us he
was beaten by a gang in Red Hook who
he tried to buy drugs from on his way
to visit his brother in Staten Island.

We had sex after explaining to the
maniac on the floor above us that Red
Hook isn't on the way to Staten
Island and we had to get the super to
turn off the water in his tub and the
super is going to recommend that the
maniac on the floor above us, who
sees devils living in many corners of
his life, be evicted immediately for
nonpayment of rent and for constantly
coming home from Red Hook bleeding
from the face.

We had sex after an attempted
assassination of the president of the
United States.

We would have sex after returning
from Westchester where her parents
lived and inspired tears and had the
power to reduce her to the status of
an undisciplined punk with no respect
for their values and customs, who had
sex out of wedlock with a Puerto
Rican, in many locations and quite frequently.

We would have sex without protection.

We would have sex while children
starved, racists ran for office, war
was waged on the poor, exotic and
never-to-be-duplicated forms of life
were deleted, fundamentalists
dictated the terms of our living, the
hoarding classes perfected devious
and more efficient ways to horde and
the country drowned in capital,
optimism, envy and bullshit.

We would have sex when we didn't feel like it.

We would have sex after bad dreams.

We would have sex after burying our
parents and grandparents, while work
became more and more meaningless, and
friends questioned their marriages.

We would have sex while our children asked about sex.

We would have sex in spasms, in
waves, in circles, in small
violences, in secret ecstasies, in
patient waiting, in doubts, in
forgotten languages, in extreme
loneliness, in promises kept, in
wishes left unacknowledged, in ritual
fantasy—in peril and in peace.

CAMILIA SANES

I was known as quiet and studious.

My glasses embarrassed me
and I hid them often
and suffered the anger of my mother
who also wore glasses,
but she was proud of hers.

She was studious too.
She covered the house in books.
She read in the bathtub
and read to me every night of my life.
Long, great, hard books full of characters
and interweaving chapters
and sentences with so many commas and colors.
Friendly books with heroes.

I listened so hard.
I settled into my bed
trying to melt into the sheets,
trying to surround my body
with the warm mattress.
I don't think I really heard the words.
I didn't need to.

The words were like waves on the beach,
lifting me softly,
tumbling me in crazy rapids,
pushing me under for moments
of brief, airless, gasping terror,
then delivering me up again—

up to air,
up to sunlight,
up to the light in my small bedroom
and my mother's shape on the bed,
her out-of-style glasses
glistening with mischief and hard work.

The words washed away
the stress of nasty girls
who excluded me on the playground.
The words washed away
the tests that I hated and failed,
despite my glasses and my studying.

The words were invisible fingers
my mother employed
to hold me close and warm,
to squeeze my brain a little tighter,
to hold in firm embrace
my throbbing lungs,
my mighty muscled heart.

She was a dreamer.
She dreamed worlds and they appeared
next to the bathtub in hardcover.

Sometimes I didn't know
if I was really there.
Sometimes I wondered
if maybe she dreamed me too.
She needed a little daughter
who looked and acted like she did
and she forced me by incredible
willpower through the fallopian tubes

of her mind
and squeezed me out of her imagination,
blue and bawling,
complete with glasses and gratitude,
asleep at her side in our cozy bed,
dreamer and dream together. ⎯⎯⎯

ANNE O'SULLIVAN

Um.
Let's see.
I learned a few things while I was there . . .
over there . . .
wherever there is.
Was.
Is that what I should talk about?
I don't know if I can talk about no sex.

Okay.
What I learned.
Um.
Children?
Children contain all the necessary ⎤
wisdom to create a civilization. ⎦

Um.
Evil is unexplainable. ⎤
So don't even try. ⎦
If you suddenly don't understand the
words and actions of your family
members or best friends, think drugs.
Money fucks relationships.
That one's obvious.

All straight men are attracted to all
straight women all the time.
Rice and beans are better than potatoes.

You will never be able to fully
forgive your parents.
Dreams are the Earth's telepathy.
Eat as much as you can, a famine is
coming. Baby boomers have completely
run out of Great Ideas.
Strong moonlight is healing.
Let people know when you're in love
with them. Lies make your lips smaller.
Pay bills a day late.
Strangers are opportunities for mischief—

take advantage.
Paint a classroom.
Wash all your dishes by hand and
contemplate the value of water.
Sins are man-made.
Never trivialize the Supreme Being.
Good prayer is biofeedback.
You can't love a child too much.
Don't fuck with people who believe in
you. Anger is contagious,
so be careful who you sleep with.
Rice and beans are better than pasta.
Grow one edible fruit or vegetable to
supplement your income.
Baseball is a game not a metaphor.
Life is neither a dream nor a cabaret.
You don't have to choose between
passion and security.

There are many parallel Americas and
the rich have the better one.
Listen to your jealousy.
I was shot in the head and I think,
to satisfy the Second Amendment, all
Americans should own one eighteenth-century
musket and that's it.
Religion and spirituality are two
completely different things in America.

DAWNN LEWIS

Night of the unrest,
I was at a screening in Santa Monica.
The week before,
the radio was stolen out of my car.
At the screening, there's no TV,
nobody really knows what's up.
I leave the screening around eleven o'clock,
with no idea what's happening,
except I knew the verdict came down
and I'm feeling real sick to my stomach at this point.
And I'm driving back to Pasadena on the 10 . . .
and I see this black towering mass
on the freeway right in front of me,
a huge, black funnel, like, I'm not shittin' you,
someone just let some evil genie out of a bottle,
and I'm all, "Fuck me, it's a tornado!
There's a fucking tornado in L.A.!"
And I'm freaking out!
Then I see *another* one, next to it, *another* one.
Then I realize: no; that's smoke; the city's on fire;
and then I see it's only burning on my *right*, *south* of the 10,

in the black part of town.
And when I understand this . . .
I feel those tornadoes lifting up my car
and spinning me in space and
I'm part of this terrifying wind blowing all our hopes away:
the firestorm in the neighborhood
full of old hatreds,
left over anxiety from the Watts riots,
years of blame and disappointment,
swirling all together in a huge funnel of air,
black and thick, taking me to some anti-Oz
where the yellow brick road's red with blood
and tornadoes don't stop spinning,
and they spin continuously,
to this day, to this minute,
and all I want to do is spin around,
throwing curses and venom in every direction,
at everyone who's forgotten . . .

RICK COCA

I was waiting outside the house
for almost an hour.
My *novia* was working in this house.
Anglo family.
Watching their children.
They were supposed to get back by 11:30.

It was past midnight.
We didn't think they'd want me in their house
so I waited in the car on the street in front.

I drove a small and dented Toyota.
The neighborhood was rich.

Big houses, not too much happening at night.
Dead and dark.
Sometimes you see coyotes looking for food.
Or an opossum crawling across the road.
They are very slow animals.
No wonder so many of them die.
You see their guts spattering all over the road.
They are not pretending then.

Animals fascinate me.
Where I grew up you lived with animals.
You understood their habits.
You paid attention to what they needed
or they would die.
If they die, you die.
I watched them being born!
I got used to blood and birth.
I understood the great variety of shit
in the animal kingdom.

My mother taught me to kill chickens
with my hands.
You grab them around the neck and then
you spin them around.
They struggle and some of them can really cut you bad
if you're not careful.
When I was a child I loved to kill them like that.

Later I butchered pigs.
I pretended the pig was a condemned man,
a murderer, rapist, with no soul,
who never repented,
and spit at the priest giving him Last Rites

and mocked the sacraments
and the family of the victim,
boasted he raped little girls.
I held the knife tight.
Looked at the struggling, confused pig.
Imagined the rapist or the unrepentant murderer
and I was chosen by the court to execute this scum.
I never smiled.
I never let the pig's—
I mean the prisoner's—
screams distract me.
I plunged the knife into its soft throat—
far as it could go—
and I cut and cut and the animal screamed
like a man and I imagined
the bleeding prisoner
finally understanding the meaning of his crimes,
repenting, fearing God,
believing in God's wisdom,
God's punishment, which I carried out.
I was the messenger of God,
the word of God, I said,
"Don't kill," "Don't rape," "Don't sin". . .
I was the terrible messenger
and this knife was my message.
I took myself very seriously
when I was ten years old.

I feared nothing except goats.
I wouldn't kill goats.
I wouldn't come near them.
They have haunted eyes: God protect me!
They seem like the reincarnated souls of madmen.
When they cry out, it sounds like your name.

I would practically shit myself in fear.
I begged my father to get rid of the goats.

One day—I cried in front of my father
and he was so offended
he hit me over the head
with the handle of a machete
and told me to stop acting like a girl.
He locked me in the goats' pen
for a day to punish me
and those madmen brayed
and shouted at me,
told me their stories,
their past lives.
It was hard to make out their words.
But I understood enough.

One had set his hair on fire.
One had eaten rats.
One believed he was Pope John XXIII.
One had sat in a room twelve years,
sitting in his own shit,
dreaming of space travel.

I screamed at them to stop talking to me.
Worried, my father let me out at dinner time—
he was going to make me spend the night there,
but changed his mind,
afraid a night with those madmen
would drive me so insane everyone
would pity him for having an insane child in his family—
and my father hated people's pity
more than he hated having a sissy son.

I wiped my eyes and walked out the pen.
I never cried in front of him again.

To this day, animals fail to move me
with their dying, their breeding—so what?
The coyotes hurrying through these
big-shot Anglo neighborhoods at night,
ignoring me in my Toyota as I wait for my girlfriend—so what?

I waited out there nearly an hour.
I was low in my seat,
thinking of my youth in Nicaragua
among animals.
It was dark and quiet.
I was about to fall asleep.
Far away I heard a car.
It wasn't going fast.
I thought, No.
I didn't move.
I could feel the sweat in my hands.
My asshole tightening.
The car had very bright headlights
and it stopped right behind me,
engine running,
lights shining into my car,
I thought, No.

I waited and decided to sit up.
The police lights shot on,
red-and-blue swirls colliding in my face,
my stomach turning into boiling water,
my mouth dry.
Two men got out.
One of them shined a flashlight in my face.

I waited.
The other cop stood behind the first
and he waited.
Man's eyes were cold.
Man's eyes stared right into me.
I turned my head
and wouldn't look in his eyes
as the other one told me to get out of the car very,
    very slow,
hand on his gun,
the night very still,
coyotes long gone,
scared away by the action, instinctual.
I stood there
and explained what my business was
on this street
and one of the cops looked at me
the way I used to look at the pigs
I was about to slaughter,
cold, convinced of my higher duty,
the spokesman of God,
the messenger,
the punisher,
the death-bringer.

MARICELA OCHOA

I wanted to be a ballerina or an astronaut.

In my imagination, day after day,
I practiced dancing on the moon.
If there was life on Mars, I would waltz with it.

Before the accident, I kept a journal.
I drew pictures of other Life Forms.
Creatures with sticky tentacles and multiple eyes—
I drew rock monsters, worms with intelligence, plasma jellies
    with attitude—
and all of them had rhythm.
They could salsa!
They could tango!
They could do splits!

I learned that dancing on Jupiter is a challenge.
Heavy gas, lots of gravity—
good for slow dancing.
But you can't jitterbug there.

Before I was paralyzed,
my body could do almost anything.
I learned movements instantly.
My body was a library of dance styles.
On long interplanetary voyages
I imagined leading the crew in the Charleston,
the minuet, the merengue, the hula and the mashed potato.

Wars between rival civilizations
in the dark corners of space
would be averted
because my body
would translate between species—
and one-eyed creatures of one world
would read the words
of ten-armed creatures of another world
by following the movements of my hips.

My legs would speak of peace.
My torso would convince

skeptical generals of warlike peoples
that love is a greater conqueror than conquest.
My body would be a peace treaty.
My limbs would be paragraphs on disarmament.
My eyes would be the signatures
of diverse universal leaders.

And my toes would be the footnotes.

MICHI BARALL

I have so many questions, I don't know where to begin. Let's start with the research I was doing. So is it true? About the river of galaxies? I have to know this!

The expanding universe—okay?—expands uniformly in all directions according to the Big Bang theory. But then we discovered that the expanding universe wasn't so uniform after all. That, in fact, there is a river of galaxies heading off in the direction of Virgo—a massive flow of galaxies being sucked into *one direction*, completely at odds with the Big Bang theory. All over the scientific community people were freaking out.

Then a few years ago, my colleagues and I—we called ourselves the Seven Samurai—we discovered that a *Massive Great Attractor* is pulling a quarter of the known universe—a two hundred million light year region of space—at the speed of 1.2 million miles per hour. *Pulling* it.

Why? What's out there? Are they giving away immortality? Is it something really bright and shiny? Is it something musical? An astronomical Pied Piper hauling a quarter of the universe's known mass in one direction? I mean, how good can it be? Or is it something sinister? Is something out there eating matter? Is the universe flat? Should we fear, like the sailors of antiquity, the horizon—because there's a point beyond which we can't go? A falling off point? I gotta know this!

I had a thing happen to me; I was eight. I was in my backyard. Alone. My mother was upstairs taking a nap because the baby was finally asleep. I was playing with a sword stabbing invisible enemies.

Then the light around me changed. I dropped the sword, looked around. And something on the other side of the yard was . . . calling me—*pulling* me—to it. I don't remember well! It was a light, it was a sound like music, it was warm, it was friendly, but very stern, it was large, it was very strong, and I could feel my body leaning that way. I looked down, and the grass, too, was leaning that way. The air seemed to be blowing in that one direction. I took a step toward this thing, this Attraction. I noticed my soccer ball rolling toward it. Getting faster the further it got from me. I wanted to cry. Each step, it felt a little stronger, it seemed to get a little brighter. I was starting to fight it, breathing very hard, I could hear myself crying, really crying hard. I noticed all the trees were bending in that direction, too, as if they were pointing something out to me. I called my mother's name! It was like the sound of my voice was suddenly grabbed by big hands and thrown to the other side of the yard. I saw a few of my tears leave my face and go right into the swirling eye of this Big Attraction. There was no sound but the soft music and my hard crying.

Then it stopped. The whole thing just stopped. The music, the lights, gone.

Whatever it was, had it gotten what it wanted? Did it just want a couple of my tears? The sound of my voice as I called my mother?

All my life, I've been attracted to stars and night skies, trying to understand what happened to me when I was eight: hoping, with the aid of telescopes and satellites, to hear that eerie music again and feel that warmth. I still don't know if the thing wanted to eat me or love me. I was attracted to the big dome of the planetarium—but then the shaking started and the whole structure, attracted by gravity, collapsed on me and sent me here. Attracted to the Big Questions of the universe, I think of that river of galaxies, wondering if it's pulled by the same force that nearly seduced me in my backyard, desperately needing to know if it will eat us or love us.

JOHN ORTIZ

Last year we were in Puerto Rico.
And we were on the beach.
Sun going down.
Beautiful, red, bursting sun, dropping . . .
golden coins into the ocean.
And I was eating a mango.
And it was sticky and sweet.
And Therese was rubbing my back,
real gentle, and sometimes her hand
would come down to my ass.
And someone on the beach
was playing a twelve-string mandolin
and a little girl was singing
in a high stratosphere voice,
pure and brown like her skin . . .

these golden flecks around her greenish eyes . . .
like she'd been kissed there
by the sun's miniature lips . . .
little kiss-tattoos
around the solar system of her mulatto eyes:
her voice bathing me in warm, fat notes,
ancient notes full of slavery and passion.
And I asked myself as I stood there on the beach:
why am I not happy here?
Why don't I stay here and live like this
the rest of my life?
Why, God, isn't this enough?
And I realize now—my ambition
was like a disease in my system.
This disease was commanding me
to leave paradise and kill myself
with work twenty-four hours a day.
And even if this disease destroyed me,
I had to obey it.
It would not let me go
no matter how much I drown it
in mangoes and music and sun showers.

ESTHER SCOTT

I ran for president.
No one knew me.
All my life I wanted to be president.
The apex of my life!

I went door-to-door
trying to get enough signatures
to put me on the ballot in Michigan.

Most people slammed their doors in my face.
I never got any media coverage.
But I gathered signatures.
I had a few passionate followers.

I had a message: in 1990, 13% of all voters were from families
whose incomes were under $15,000.

In 1992 that percentage had dropped to 11%.

In 1994, of all the families making less than $15,000 a year,
only 7.7% bothered to vote.

In 1989 the inequality of wealth distribution in the United
States was at a 60 year high.

Imagine what it is now!

The top 1% of families ranked by financial wealth had 48% of
all the wealth in the country.

The top 20% owned 94% of the country's wealth.

In 1989, 35% of all families of color reported zero or negative
net worth.

So I got a few hundred signatures.
I shook a few hundred hands.
In brief moments I made real connection
to real people.
I gave them a little hope.
I made their country a little better for them.
For a couple of minutes there were
a few people who could smell change in the air.
Who witnessed the unlikely birth of a new nation.

I ate a lot of red meat with the people.
Funny.
I couldn't tell if they were humoring me or not.
But I drank a few cold beers.

SAM WELLINGTON

I'm surrounded by strangers.
I'm trying to just deal.
I want answers.
I'd like to see the man in charge.
I'd like to see a schedule!
I'd like to know when I get to set the pace of events around here!

I operated a forklift.
And I had my problems with substance abuse.
Okay?
But that's all past now.
That shit's gone bye-bye as far as I'm concerned.
As far as I know doing hard drugs isn't technically a sin in the
    record books of any organized religion I'm aware of.
Last time I checked.

I partied.
Sure, I partied.
I liked to kick back, shoot the shit
with a few friends over a barbecue grill,
Coors Light in one hand, spatula in the other.
Entertain the masses.
I'd drink far more than my share.
I'd get pissed—
been known to happen.
Get a little mellow—

girls look exceptionally good, why not?
Last time I perused the holy pages,
I don't believe beer or pussy
were on the list of frowned-upon human activities.
I can say pussy if I want!

Consenting adults, of course,
I didn't chase no children,
didn't offer beer or pot to minors.
If I ended up in the arms of a married woman,
I know I wasn't breaching any kind of
earth-shattering moral responsibility.
As long as I wasn't coveting her.
I wasn't *coveting* her, I was *copulating* her.
And I didn't go for sodomy!
So you can't fault me on that line of reasoning.
And it's not like I'm some kind of Samson of the love-crowd:
my success rate's pretty single digits most times.
Usually it was drink, drink, puke, puke—crawl on hands and
    knees over cold tile—wish to God I owned a handgun so
    I could nullify the drumbeat in the whimpering bloodpools
    of my brain.
Thoughts of self-slaughter,
even if you read the fine print under this heading,
isn't the actual event and therefore not covered in this clause!

Never killed no one.
Never worshipped graven images.
Never had no pictures of Baal or Mithra or Mothra or whatev-
    er those Babylonian deities were called.
Didn't worship no cows either!
Except a couple of human ones!
Never bought Proctor and Gamble satanic products.

I've broken the law.
Sure.
Flat broke so bad one year, had to steal medicines when I got
    sick—
especially my asthma and those
inhalers are marked up to extremes,
talk about sin.
So I'd lift a few of those.
Yeah, that's theft, that's stealing,
that's, that's pretty certain, you know, no-holds-barred sinning.
You got me there.

I remember from the Bible classes,
they'd have a drawing of a quart of
milk and that's your pure, white soul.
But the sinners have little black
smudges on their quarts of milk.
And anything other than actual white
milk in that bottle was fucked.
It ruined the perfection.
And it pretty much ruined your
chances of experiencing the bliss
of heavenly reunion with the Great Creator—
though I gotta say I'm still waiting
for the bliss part to kick in here.
So I guess my thieveries are showing
up on the outer lining of my soul.
But I'll tell you how unfair that is.
I was hungry, I was having asthma attacks.
I was not greedy.
And I wasn't packing anything.

And, you know, these were Man's laws
I was breaking and I really do think

something as small and temporary as
Man's laws have no real long-term
effect on something as total and
permanent as the human soul.
That's just my opinion.
The opinion of a working man.
I know I can look right into the
terrible eyes of our Lord Jesus and
be secure in the knowledge that the
smudges on my eternal soul are slight
and unimportant and simply the wages
of living in an imperfect world run
by Man and his laughable laws.
Looks like I covered most of the
territories of the known sins.

Okay, the only thing, maybe, was . . .
while my father was dying in Jersey
. . . and I couldn't go visit him.
No, it wasn't like I couldn't get
time off or I couldn't afford it or
the car died or nothing.
I just couldn't go.
Look at him in the bed.
Legless.
His right arm paralyzed from the strokes.
His power of speech eradicated.
Facial muscles uncontrollable.
Watch him staring at the television
all day long, screaming out the only
word his mouth could form: "Ma!"
Calling my mother.
Ma!
Whenever he needed her to turn him over.

Ma!
Or find him a Mets game on TV.
Ma!
Or turn off the harsh light.
Or put the picture of Lord Baby Jesus
just a little closer, Ma, just a
little closer, Ma! Ma! Ma.

Sorry, I couldn't watch this.
I didn't go.
For years.
I'd let my siblings deal with all
that shit while I continued to not
know and not investigate and not do
one blessed thing for the man,
outside of having fantasies of
killing him by suffocation and ending
the pretense, the Bible reading, the
hand clapping, the speaking in
tongues, the false hope, ending it,
ending it, for God's sakes let the
poor man die, why don't you?
Just let the poor man die.

Thou shall honor thy mother and
thy father.
Jesus.

ROBERT MONTANO

My wife . . .

. . . she gave her old clothes to a local church . . .
she knew the mailman's birthday . . .
she gave to UNICEF . . .
she sent passionate faxes to elected officials . . .
she knew the first twelve Shakespeare sonnets by heart . . .
she said good-bye to toll booth people . . .
"bye-bye toll booth person!" . . .
she returned her library books on time . . .
she visited her eternal grandmother every faithful summer . . .
the old woman's one remaining pleasure . . .
incontinent, toothless, unhappy . . .
connecting her granddaughter, through endlessly repeated
    anecdotes, to the history written in her blood . . .

. . . she swore she'd buy herself a gun and shoot herself in the
    head before she'd put up with an old age like this . . .
we planned to get ancient together and do the joint-suicide
    thing . . .

. . . but there was a guy . . .

. . . a guy who washes car windows in front of the bank in our
    neighborhood . . .
young guy . . .
filthy . . .
heroin . . .
always had a skateboard . . .
she'd drive up to the bank . . .
give him a dollar to clean the windshields . . .

. . . they'd hang out and talk . . .
they did this every Saturday morning . . .
he's very good-looking . . .
despite the filth . . .

. . . she used to shoot up, so she understood . . .
I thought they were in love . . .
they had "a thing" . . .
I waited in the car as they laughed . . .
she once gave him a twenty, got in the car, crying . . .
she said, "I just heard the saddest story" . . .

. . . his new tattoo . . .
I swore it was her name surrounded by a crown of thorns . . .
the woman he couldn't have . . .
I wanted to kill this man . . .
he was pathetic . . .
smelled like a urinal . . .
she got too *close* to him . . .
I didn't want his clothes to brush her clothes . . .
came home one day . . .
there he is *in the kitchen* . . .
merrily drinking coffee . . .
he's talking to her about movies . . .
big fan of Hitchcock . . .
what the fuck is going on here? . . .
I wanted to unwind . . .
I'm stuck with this putrid drug user *in my kitchen* pontificat-
    ing about *Strangers on a Train*! . . .

. . . we fought about it that night . . .
I told her: "I come home . . .
I can't even talk to you
because this addict is monopolizing you . . .

all I want is equal rights here!" . . .
she said, "I already know what you're going to tell me" . . .
I stare at her . . .
"I *bore* you? . . .
is that it?" . . .
"no," she said quickly . . .
I didn't even stay in bed to hear more . . .
she said, "these people need me" . . .
"I don't need you?" . . .
she said, "not in the same way" . . .
"honey, I need you in profound ways" . . .
she said, "yes, I know" . . .
"you're not going to save this man" . . .

. . . I couldn't stop imagining them together . . .
I imagined them sharing a cardboard box . . .
they do it on rusted mattresses . . .
passion heightened by rusted mattress spikes stabbing their
     naked butts . . .
in fact, pain is the goal . . .

. . . I imagined they road skateboards together . . .
panhandling in front of our house . . .
all our friends staring at her . . .
and she'd look and sound happier with him than she ever
     looked and sounded with me . . .
beneath the layers of traffic soot and sidewalk dirt her eyes were
     full of wisdom and fulfillment and absolute freedom . . .
the freedom only vaguely imagined by the housebound . . .
freedom to say "fuck you" . . .
to stare at the drivers waiting for the light to change . . .
she'd challenge them: "hey you in the Lexus, are you moral?
     empathic? . . .
you think you are . . .

you tell your children you are . . .
in your prayers you boast that you are . . .
yet here I am . . .
LOOK AT ME . . .
I'm staring into the deepest tunnels of your heart and I'm not
    seeing shit . . .
you want me gone . . .
you hope I fall off the edge of the known world . . .
fall painlessly into oblivion while you drive to your
    appointments" . . .

. . . she wanted that power . . .
and that power was something she could only get from him . . .

. . . then he disappeared . . .

. . . after that we would drive together . . .
anywhere . . .
didn't matter . . .
there they were . . .
like an army of vampires, bloodless, in their rags and filth . . .
they knew about her . . .
they sought her out . . .
she radiated goodness and they wanted it . . .
they wanted to drink from her kindness like it was an ancient
    tribal river . . .
to suck her down into their limbs . . .
to own her . . .

. . . my wife . . .
actually began to disappear in front of my eyes . . .
I watched helpless as she gave away scraps of herself . . .
first the excess . . .
then the vital tissues . . .

until she disappeared completely from my sight . . .
down into the tortured piranha pit of the homeless . . .

. . . away from me . . .
happy . . .
alive . . .

and finally at home.

VANESSA MARQUEZ

I caused the Northridge earthquake.
Me! How did I do it? How do I know?
Because the night of the earthquake
I was in the Northridge Hospital.
I was paralyzed from the waist down
from a car accident I got into on the 10.
I was in the hospital for months.
I wasn't improving.
I couldn't stop crying!
But the night of the earthquake,
I was lying in bed,
trying with all my heart and soul
to move my useless legs.
And you know what?
I did! I moved my legs—
and just at that very same second,
the earthquake happened!
I made the whole earth shake with my tiny legs!
Houses fell.
Mountains shifted.
Continents kissed and divorced!
Cracks went down deeper than any hell

I could imagine!
And I did that! Me.
All by myself.

And that terrified me.
And I saw what I did
to all those people and houses
and I cried and asked God to forgive me.
I just didn't know, God!
I was humbled and inspired
and now I can walk.
Now I can walk.

A N A   O R T I Z

There's somebody . . . I don't know who he is . . . I want to take
this time to apologize to him. I don't know your name. I don't
know what you look like.

You were in the Bronx about seven years ago. Let's see, it was
outside the 180th Street stop on the 2, close to one in the morn-
ing. I don't remember the name of the street anymore.

But right there, under the elevated tracks, at the intersection, on
the left as you go east, one night seven years ago . . . I saw you.

It was very dark there. All I wanted to do was to get home. So
I'm walking fast 'cause I hate that street and I almost didn't see
you. But I did see you.

Two men were holding you by the arms and they where slam-
ming you headfirst into the front of a parked car. I couldn't see

your face. The two guys were laughing. You fell to the ground. I only watched for a second.

I got out of there as fast as I could. I went home. I didn't call the cops. I didn't call for help. I didn't jump in to break it up. I didn't go back later to see if you were okay. I didn't do nothing but run. Protect my ass.

For a second I actually convinced myself that you guys were playing some kind of game, maybe you were just kids.

I'm sorry. If you're out here. If you're hearing this. I was the one who walked away that night and left you there and I haven't been able to stop thinking about you in seven years and I thought, here, now, this would be the time to say I was sorry. This would be the time.

Please forgive me, sir. Please forgive me.

CARLO ALBAN

I see some gods on the moon.
I also see it moving, just a little,
let's pretend my hand is the moon,
it's going like this.

The moon has too much light.
I think it's the gods.
They're having fires there.
The light shoots!
It goes past all the black air in space
and hits my eyes and I feel the hot too,
the hot light from the gods on the moon.

I can't hear them talking,
they're too far away.
I think they're mad at us.
I think they want to blow us up.
They talk whispering.
If we went in the clouds with machine guns
and arrows
we could kill them.
We hate them.
The gods have no eyes.
They left their eyes at home.
Their hearts are squish and their
blood is really smooth and warm.
It feels like this.

They waited a long time.
They watch us.
They know everything we do.
Some day we're all going to get real sick
and have a disease
and be really dead, everybody.
Like all the dinosaurs and pterodactyls did.
But faster.
In one night we'll all die and lie down in bed
and fall asleep and be dead.
That's when the gods on the moon
will find their eyes and come down to earth,
and take the whole place over.

JOHN VARGAS

I was obsessed with the veins in her neck!
I could see her blue thick veins
running from her chin down to her chest,
along the velvet hills of her skin,
these arteries full of rich, dark blood,
twisting around like the friggin' streets of L.A.
Every time I drove I felt myself traveling the veins
of her neck, getting lost in her hot Cuban bloodstream . . .

But it was so stupid because
it was so fucking doomed because
even if I wasn't married to her sister,
even if I was single,
I was all wrong for her!
She's into bad boys!
Men with prison records!
Chain smokers! Tattoos!
I didn't even have facial hair!
I hated loud noises!
She liked ex-heroin addicts!
There's a certain romance to men like that!
A mystique!
There was absolutely no friggin' chance for me!
It was pathetic!
It was sickening!
I was disgusted with my life!
I went out west to fucking escape
and my fucking life decided to follow me!
I wasn't a man!

God help me,
I was a parody of a man.

SVETLANA EFREMOVA

I would breathe against the window and watch the thin white cloud my breath made on the glass and I would take a finger and write an X in the mist. Then I would move ever-so-slightly left or right and I would exhale again and make another small cloud on the glass and again I would make an X. I did this until I had covered the entire window in that room with the white anxious smoke of my lungs. Then I would go to the next window and start over and make small Xs, row upon row, small exact Xs, engraved in the temporary surface my breath made on the cold window panes.

I wouldn't even look outside. I never took my eyes off the small X, then the next virgin spot on which there wasn't an X. And even if I had wanted to look outside, it would have been point-less to look, as the other side of the window was inches thick with dirt and car exhaust and pigeon shit. The light that pene-trated that window was a urine-colored little spit of light, a little piss of light fighting the compacted air and finally leaking into the room, yellow and anxious, like a diabetic's piss.

There were nine windows in the room and nine is the number of redemption.

I don't know why I made so many Xs. I was amazed by this activity. I couldn't stop. Not even when they brought the food. Little trays with neatly wrapped sandwiches, which I ignored until I was nearly starving, but ate quickly because I didn't want to stop making Xs on those silent nine windows. In fact hunger only heightened my desire, motivated me, gave me a heroic rea-son to continue the punishment, the shameful, secret ritual that had locked its iron jaws around my mind.

I began to despise myself for my weakness: it wasn't a voice, or a pair of hands, but some force had seized me and all my cursing and rebellious fantasies were wasted on it. Superior and inexhaustible it commanded, yes, commanded me to continue.

Why did I obey? I loved food. I loved going to the bathroom. I loved living in my dreams. I loved exploring sin, but only in my imagination. Outside of my imagination I was terrified of sin and would never commit one and I'd follow every rule, man-made or dictated by God, no matter how absurd, I listened, I followed. Fear motivated me and I never strayed from the narrow pathway leading from birth to death. I let pleasures elude me. I let people walk away from me, free of my fantasies of them, innocent of my deeply buried desires and dreams, the twisting, fantastic, highly plotted, improbable living dreams in which I satisfied every need and never paid for it, never lost a lover, never felt guilt, never apologized. I turned my back on everything in order to make little miniature Xs on the surface of great industrial windows, tightly interconnected X-patterns as elaborate and lovely as the Book of Kells.

What was I trying to make? What code was I trying to break?

At times I was vaguely aware of others in the room with me. I didn't know if they were real or ghosts. I was aware of distant voices, detached and clinical, voices that freeze your blood and incense your mind, voices I tried to ignore as I covered those vast windows in Xs. I wanted to stop and address the voices. To turn around and viciously insult whoever it was who spoke to me in such rude and disrespectful ways. But I found I couldn't turn around. I couldn't stop making Xs in the windows. Night after night, sleepless, nearly starved, I continued my work in light that obscured my vision and among voices that confused my hearing.

I imagined my fists breaking through the window. I imagined throwing my only chair through the window. I imagined great pure sunlight storming into the room: then air—pure air! And, then, space beyond the window, space to walk and breathe and really live. I imagined eating food again and having lovely bowel movements and rerunning my sexual fantasies and getting an apartment and a car and maybe a temp job in a secure office, some old corporation that would take good care of me.

I would like that. I would develop as a human being in that scenario. I would acquire a small selection of elite books. The great thoughts of mankind. I'd buy CDs and listen to the latest tunes. I would flourish within the context of new friendships. People would bring me news of distant places. All would find my story of the room and the Xs appalling and fascinating. I would develop a reputation as an appalling and fascinating individual. No one at the corporation would suspect the depth of the quiet and loyal little functionary in the next cubicle. Storage of so many secrets would only enhance my mental powers. I have been a wanderer, an explorer of the twisting pathways of the mind. My passport is stamped by nations grotesque and wonderful.

Over and over again I would be aware of my moral superiority. Over and over again . . . over and over again . . . over and over again . . . as I made my Xs. As I made my Xs in my urine-colored room I realized how stupid these fantasies were. How abject and cruel. My fantasies made me sick. And in that sickness I found a strange liberation.

A strange liberation is what you gave me.

JESSICA HECHT

The air killed me.
I was sensitive—
but not any more
than the average person, I think.
I liked to breathe.
Breathing was a good thing.

I had an office on Wilshire and La Brea.
The Asahi Building, eleventh floor,
a balcony that went three-quarters
the way around the building,
you had a view east, south and west.
Spectacular sometimes when the air was invisible.
But that was rare:
most times it clung to the ground
like mustard gas,
like some kind of white moss,
like a viral infection
along the tissues of your moist lungs—
like the kiss of death,
like a bad chance,
a freak ghost,
a haunting,
polluted Karma,
warmed over holistic spiritual bullshit.

I would stand on my balcony
trying to see vistas
and downtown structures
and only see the brown death-clouds
of our automotive suicide

and I'd stand there
coughing and cursing like a tubercular mad freak,
face all red, phlegm the color of unsanitary blood—
I could taste multinational oil giants
in the unhappy folds of my violated tastebuds;
I could taste Middle East petro-dollars
in my hacking dry wheezing breath
and I'd cough and I'd curse
like some twentieth century version of Captain Ahab—
I swear I could feel one of my legs turning into wood—
ranting against the visible air,
shaking my fist at the death clouds,
spitting at the smudged and indifferent horizon,
straining to see the so-called beauty
in the so-called mountain ranges
and my eyes slamming into that beige curtain,
that soiled atmosphere,
and I'd curse its opacity and its density;
I'd curse its weight
and its love of gravity and street level;
I'd curse its vile and undefeatable smugness,
its certainty that in this minuscule dance of death
we had together, it—not I—would prevail;
it—not I—would be writing
the obituary for the morning paper.

That was a Monday morning
I had those thoughts.

I went home at six o'clock.
I sat in the eye-clogging, spirit-stomping traffic
traveling the four miles from the Asahi Building to my home in
    Los Feliz
in about what seemed like

and couldn't have possibly been less than
one solid hour of nerve-crushing,
soul-spattering numbness.

I got home.
I was in my home.
I was contemplating a wide variety
of Trader Joe's frozen delights.
What will it be tonight? I asked myself.

The frozen Trader Joe's Chicken Burrito?
Or the frozen Trader Joe's Veggie Biryani?

I was staring at my freezer
contemplating another exciting night
of microwave, television and insomnia . . .
when I notice a bright red smudge
out of the corner of my eye.
I turned to look at it.
It was a pane of glass in the kitchen window
reflecting light.

It was the kind of red
you only dream about
when you dream about absolutes.
The red from the inside of your corpuscles
or the center of a volcano's burning stomach
or the red of infinite anger
or the deepest passion.

I realized it was reflecting the light
coming in from the living room.
I went to the living room
and looked out the big bay windows.

The windows that face west.
The sun was going down.

How do I explain this?
The dirty air created the most—
it was the most fantastic—
no, it, it, it was the most spectacular—
no, it was an explosion of oranges and reds—
no, that doesn't do it,
that doesn't say how
fuckingly fuckingly fuckingly beautiful
that sunset was that evening
hovering like red liquid over the west,
the air dust twisting and bending
the rays of final sunlight
like the shapes in a Calder mobile,
or the ornate lines
of the Shahnama-yi Shahi,
those rays of light
were twisted and bent
beyond imaginable wavelengths
and color patterns:
I saw lava in the sky,
I saw lung tissue,
I saw rose petals,
I saw bloodied mountains,
I saw red rainbows . . .
and I saw it change
and undulate and tease
and I said to myself,
I gotta go outside
and get a better look at this,
I gotta have one really good experience
in this no-exit day.

So I walked down the steps to the driveway
to get a better look at the sunset.

At that very exact moment
my next door neighbor Lourdes,
a woman about my age,
with a waterfall of churning black hair
and eyes like big radar dishes,
she was coming out of her apartment
to look at the pollution-created,
spectacular, massively red display of,
I don't know: pure glory.
And the both of us
just stood there long minutes
watching this sky-thing
changing and rotating
and I didn't even notice she was there
and we didn't notice each other
as the sun disappeared
and the sky darkened
and I swear I'd never seen this woman in my life
and it turns out we've been neighbors
for three years
and she lives with two roommates
and it's a little crazy
and lately the walls have been closing in
and I explained I lived alone
and my walls are closing in, too
and wasn't that the most incredible looking sunset
any person has ever seen?
And isn't it funny we both decided
it was so beautiful
we had to venture outside
to get a really good look at it?

215

And why don't you come over
and have some
frozen Trader Joe's Calamari in Oyster Sauce with me?
And sure that would be fun.

And she came over
and we played my old Lightning Hopkins records
I haven't listened to in half a century
and she told me stories of loss and sadness
and she cried on my shoulder
and I cried on hers
and we exchanged
fleeting, tender fingertip touches
and I do believe
that was the very last time
I ever cursed the air pollution in my life.

GENO SILVA

I grew up with a guy who is now
the most famous TV producer of all time.
Same neighborhood.
Same girlfriends, everything,
and that motherfucker stole the Fonz off me.
We came to Hollywood the same time.
I had an idea for a show.
I said to him two words: "The fifties."
That's all I said!
And, before you know it,
this cocksucker's got *Happy Days* on the air!
He steals the Fonz from me!
My creation!
The voice, the leather jacket, the hair,
the look, I *did* the "look,"

everything, the cool control Fonzie had,
the way he could just slice through a situation
like a red hot razor blade,
the antihero loneliness,
the outsider metaphysic,
the cleft chin,
all of that, all of that was mine,
and the motherfucker stole it from me
and made a fucking fortune
while I found myself sitting in an office
with a Jew with plugs in his head
pitching to Hispanics!

ANTOINETTE ABBAMONTE

There were three boys.
One on each arm.
They pulled my arms back and it hurt.
I couldn't get loose.
I couldn't kick them.
They weren't very strong
but they were determined.

The third boy was in front of me
trying to dodge my kicks,
looking for an opening,
trying to get a good solid punch in
and I kept fighting
and a couple of other boys
were starting to gather
and laugh
and nobody went to get a teacher
or a parent

and when the boy in front of me
finally saw his opening
he punched me right in the chest
and I felt my head exploding
as if all the blood from his punch
was rushing right up into my face.

I could feel my mouth opening
and saliva coming out of it
and the laughter was even stronger
after that
and I looked up at the school
and I could see a couple of girls
looking down at me
from the second floor window
and they weren't moving or anything,
I think one of them was shaking her head no,
but no one was rushing down
to save me
and that's when I understood
the depth of the conspiracy against me,
and I started to laugh,
and the next time I looked up
at the second floor of the school,
I could see myself
looking down at myself,
not moving,
like I was another co-conspirator,
maybe even the worst one,
maybe the leader,
looking down at myself,
passive,
holding hands with the cold girls at my side,
just slowly, slowly shaking my head no.

KARENJUNE SANCHEZ

I'm sorry.
I'm just a little freaked-out at the moment.
I thought I was going somewhere else.
I thought—
because my father was black
and my mother was Hawaiian—
I'd be going somewhere else.

I'm twenty-eight.
I was born and raised in El Paso.
My father was the king of hardware and lumber.

There was a hole in the floor next to the bed.
It was very black.
My mother and father were still very poor—
before Pop became king of hardware and lumber.
We moved into this little house on the West Side.
We weren't there long.
In any case, my father filled that hole
the next day.
But my first night in that house,
I slept in a bed next to that hole in the floor
that was black and deep and quiet.

The first one to climb out of that hole
in the floor called himself Ace Man.
He was a card player from San Antonio
who died in a car accident
the day he quit his job for Bekins
and was speeding through Oklahoma
to see a new girlfriend—

a woman whose furniture he moved himself.
Ace Man had long ears and a tiny mustache
and was half-Mexican, half-Hopi.
I was eight years old and we played cards
for hours and he always beat me.

He cried out loud for his lost love
and how he never got to live with her
and how unfair it is to get killed
the day your freedom arrives
and you're on the road
and the radio's playing "Free Bird"
and the earth seems endless
and the people in it seem slightly less evil.

His friends eventually came out of the hole too:
they had funny names like
Little Finger and Clay and Smokes and Chieftain and Lagrimas
and Sparky
and all of them were mixed bloods
of some kind or another
and coming from different
and conflicting cultures
they didn't know what afterlife to go to
so they hung around this narrow hole in El Paso
for the rest of time
and they all had tales of loss and regret
and told jokes
because the loss and regrets didn't get them down
and they knew how to party
and forget their pain,
and they gave me advice
on how to live in the world
and be myself

and fight my fights,
and see the unusual in the usual,
and turn darkness into light and laughter,
and even with tears in their eyes
they knew how to laugh,
and sometimes the saddest ones
laughed the loudest,
and I thanked those imperfect souls
and I kissed each one good night
and each one slipped back
into the hole in the floor
and the next day my father
covered it up forever with cement.

And that's where I always thought I'd end up:
in a covered-up hole in a bedroom floor
in El Paso, Texas.

YUSEF BULOS

Three days in the city.

Day One. I'm walking up Hollywood Boulevard with my son. We're taking pictures of the stars on the sidewalk. Trying not to stare at the people. A man with a hat made of television parts. Homeless women picking scabs. Teenagers so thin they disappear like the sideways view of the rings of Saturn. Scientologists in neat blue uniforms walking briskly to their nautical salvation. In Dayton you just don't see these variations. A couple of limos whispering past us. A few times I thought I recognized someone from something. Day One in the city.

We stop at a big candy store. My son has died and gone to heaven. He buys little packets of false tattoos. Kids wear them all the time. I'm dreading what forms of brilliant rebellion he'll be into by the time he's a teenager. He puts a little *Jurassic Park* tattoo on his arm and begs me to put a tattoo on my arm. I didn't want to. Felt silly, of course.

But this was the first time in six months that he and I had spent an entire day together. Every second of the day was just him and me. Asks me a million "why" questions, it's that phase. I can see more of myself in him than ever before. Recognize my own reactions.

It wasn't always like this. I resented his birth. It was unexpected, unplanned. I went into a nosedive. I fretted about money so obsessively I went into counseling. I fought with my wife. I hated waking up each morning. I looked longingly at younger, unattached women and dreamed of unattachment. I would hold my newborn son and feel nothing. His crying grated on me. I had recurring fantasies in which I ran away and was never heard from again.

Then one night, it was two or three in the morning, and his crying woke me up and I told my wife I would give him a bottle. The house was silent. Only one light burned near us. I was barely awake. I held my son in the living room—it was only a few seconds before that miracle happened—and it was suddenly as if I had just awakened from a deep and troubling sleep—and I was instantly aware that I had a son.

A son.

I was looking at him as if I had never seen him before and in that second, I remember it so vividly even now, in that second I remember falling deeply in love with him—it was the first and only time in my entire life that I actually experienced the "fall" of falling in love—a swift endless drop, wind blowing in my face, down a perfectly delicious abyss . . . and I just . . . I couldn't control myself . . . I held him . . . and cried with him and I didn't want to let go. Not ever. Not for another second of my life.

Anyway. There we were on Hollywood Boulevard. In this labyrinthine candy store and he wants me to put this scorpion tattoo on my arm. Finally, I relent. I apply the temporary tattoo to my forearm. A big, green scorpion, vivid and nasty: it looks very convincing.

We walk out onto the boulevard, looking into absurd little lingerie stores, trying to explain to this little boy what that's for, trying not to stand out in general.

Suddenly a couple of young men approach us. Hispanic boys. They're very young and their heads are shaven and they wear long, baggy white T-shirts, baggy pants: chocolate complexions, dark eyes, good-looking boys, but hardened, their mouths were set in this frown, it looked permanent, as if they could easily break out in tears any second—and I rapidly tried to imagine their fathers—you know how the mind works: what do their fathers do, what do they think of these strong-looking young men with the permanently sad faces. I know their fathers must have experienced the fall I experienced with my son—so how could they possibly let these vulnerable little boys out of their sight? How could we have gotten to this moment of confrontation and implied violence? And they're looking at me very hard and they point to the child's tattoo of the scorpion on my arm and say something very quietly to me in Spanish. I don't understand what it is. Then one of them points to his forearm—he has the tattoo of a spider on his arm. And I don't understand any of this and my radar is going, "Get the hell out of there. Get out now!" And I try to move on, and they won't let me go on, and my son's crying, and finally the shorter of the two looks at my son and notices his *Jurassic Park* tattoo and realizes my scorpion is just a toy and not a real tattoo and I'm not in some rival gang— like who could believe that? The Dayton white guy gang? And this young man laughs so hard and loud—laughs with relief— I laugh, too, and he says, *"Que vida mas loca."* "Sorry, mister; whatta crazy life," in lilting, accented English and moves on.

Day Two—imagine my surprise: I'm crossing a street in Beverly Hills, don't watch my step because I'm eyeing an extraordinary blond in a top they would have prosecuted her in Dayton for, and a limo plows right into me at top speed, sending me to the intensive care unit at Cedar Sinai Hospital.

Day Three and here I am.

Can you tell me how to get word to my son, please? I want to tell him not to worry about me.

FELICITY JONES

They think I lied. I didn't lie! I had an active imagination but I didn't lie about this. It was a brain tumor! Jesus Christ!

The deadline had come and gone. I had finished the script, I really had. But it still didn't work. It needed tweaking. I told them down at Universal that it was almost ready. Give me a couple of weeks to tweak the stupid thing.

It was a genre picture. I had never done a genre picture before. New rules I had to learn. Very strict ones. Movie haiku. I held my breath and went for it. Stretched myself.

I always take my time. I'm slow. Sue me but everyone in the business knows that going into it and if you can't deal with it, don't fucking hire me!

So I missed the deadline. No one panics. Not yet. We agree on another deadline. That one comes and goes. Tempers under control, okay good. Another deadline. My manager is now starting to crack at the seams. Pieces of him are starting to fall off. The Universal people are getting ugly.

Look, I had a reputation for being excellent at my craft. Then I finished the thing and started having a brain tumor.

I called the studio. The script is close I said but I can't finish it because I have a brain tumor. They thought I lied. I didn't lie! I didn't! I could feel it throbbing in my cranium. It was like I was having a baby in my head. Like Athena was pounding the inside of my face with her big Bronze Age spear and this tumor started assuming shapes.

The shapes of an ex-husband. Screaming at me for being lazy and indecisive. Leaving me for a younger, happier version of myself. It was taking on the shape of famous people. Joan of Arc was being burned at an imaginary stake in my mind every night. I could hear the fire in my sleep. I could smell the smoke. The doctor said phantom smells were the first sign of a brain tumor. But it was the screaming that convinced me.

It wasn't my screaming. It was the screaming of the brain tumor that had assumed the shape of Sharon Tate in my brain, this blob of extra-busy brain cells that multiplied and conquered and assumed the shape of famous victims.

I had the operation. They took the tumor out of my head. I finished the script and the studio made the movie and I was nominated for my third Academy Award. Awesome dress.

I kept the tumor. I kept it in my house. It's in the refrigerator in a Tupperware-like container. It's now in the shape of, well, oddly enough, me. It's a little miniature me that I talked to and got advice from and all the neighbors and agents in town and actors who owed their careers to me thought I was crazy. But I wasn't. I didn't lie.

My tumor got on the phone and lied for me.

DORIS DIFARNECIO

I heard the truck's engine.
It was loud.
But not as loud as the wind.
A tornado wind!

I was in the back of the truck.
I was wearing Papa's old army jacket,
big and soft, smelled like him,
the sweat from his travel,
the sweat from his work,
picking oranges and artichokes.
His jacket was alive with memories
of his labors and the sweat mixed in
with the sugar and tears of all those places.
The place by the tracks,
by the slaughterhouse,
at the edge of town:
places where nobody else would live.

We crossed a lot of borders in a truck.
Since before I was born.
Following the seasons,

the rhythms of vegetables, our masters;
little plants told us where to live and when,
and Papa listened and obeyed
and kept his mouth shut
and kept out of sight
and kept listening to the orders of the crops
and we traveled to their places
and did the work we had to do
to keep them alive
and keep America fed
and we obeyed the laws,
all the laws, we had to be careful.

And the truck was full of people that night:
a few strangers we didn't know,
also migrants, also going north.

Papa stopped for them:
I don't know why—
he never does that.

They all got into the truck with me
and Mama and Papa
and we drove north
and then the police followed us.
Papa wouldn't stop.
Maybe the strangers in the truck were afraid.
They must have told him not to stop,
to go faster, and maybe he didn't want
to look weak in their eyes
and we went faster, faster,
and the wind was louder and colder
and the truck's engine was faint,
like it had left me behind . . .

and I was flying through the night air,
flying like a man-eating spirit,
flying with the demons and unlucky ghosts
of the freeway . . .
and the police wouldn't go away;
they pushed Papa faster . . .
and Papa tried a U-turn . . .
and I remember flying into a storm.

When the storm ended,
my mama and papa were gone.
The storm had turned my family to rain.
And the rain fell to the earth.
They disappeared in the thirsty earth
so they could feed the plants
who ruled their lives. Gone.

KEVIN JACKSON

I was looking down at the ocean. I was nervous. The ocean didn't frighten me. It was the sharpshooters. They patrolled the beach every half hour. Through the walls of the prison they could be heard telling obscene jokes. Sometimes they were so bored they would take target practice on the seagulls. They'd spend their entire complement of arrows on the seabirds.

No, the ocean didn't frighten me. I loved heights—my love grew stronger as the years of incarceration went by. Everything was far, far below us. The enemies who imprisoned us seemed no larger than ticks.

Our prison was the tallest structure in the country. You could see it from a hundred miles away. And everyone knew that my father and I, the most wanted criminals in the country, were trapped there, finally outsmarted, the genius and his only son contained in stone and steal, a prison even his great mind couldn't outwit. Or so they thought. My father, of course, had other plans.

At first he wouldn't even trust me with his scheme. Afraid, maybe, I'd break under torture and spill my guts. In the morning he'd draw elaborate diagrams. Study them all day. Then destroy them every night for fear the guards would find them during their periodic raids of his cell.

After a year in prison my father started asking the guards for extra candles. He was an avid reader and his eyes were going. The guards, rightfully suspicious, didn't pay him any attention. Then he went on a hunger strike—his tenth, I believe—and threatened to somehow contact the human rights groups monitoring our imprisonment—and this always freaked out the powers that be, and after nearly six months of strikes, near-deaths, stalemates, and plain old-fashioned hardball, my father got what he wanted. Two extra candles every night. I knew, instantly, that a plan was in effect.

But he was subtle. He let another six months pass.

Then my father started to complain that his shit was bloody. He requested that his diet be supplemented with grains. A month passed before he got what he wanted. A handful of grain. Then things started to pick up.

My father would put the grain on the high ledge of his one window. Inevitably a seabird would land and eat the grains. The opening was small and my father would frighten the birds so suddenly they would flap their wings while still on the ledge and inevitably the wild beating of wings against the stone window would shake feathers loose and the feathers would fall to the floor in my father's cell. This happened every day.

And it was this way, slowly, that my father collected his treasure of white feathers.

And he would melt his wax from his two extra candles and glue those feathers together and in a year's time he had fashioned identical pairs of giant wings. Then we fasted until we each weighed less than a hundred pounds.

The day came. I was looking down at the ocean. I was nervous. The ocean didn't frighten me. It was the sharpshooters. They were on the beach that day. And, again, bored and stupid, they were wasting their arrows on the hapless seabirds. When the tall one shot his very last arrow into the air, my father said, "Come on."

Through a hole in the wall my father had patiently carved out of solid rock during the years of our incarceration, we barely squeezed ourselves and our mighty wings.

As he predicted the wind was northerly. For years he had watched the patterns of the clouds, making mental notes, filed away in the great cavern of that magnificent brain, and understood the rhythms of the air, of temperature, of clouds—and predicted this day would be cloudless, no rain, no lightning, no turbulence.

We had to move fast. We climbed through the hole. We were outside for the first time in years. We strapped on our wings. The sharpshooters saw us. The fools started to shout commands! They started throwing rocks but of course the tower was much higher than any man can throw, and seconds after attaching the wings to our bodies we were lifted by a current of air.

When my feet left the ground, I gasped! I had never known such a feeling! I started to involuntarily kick the air, as if that would help me fly higher and faster, but it only dragged me down and my father told me to knock it off. "It's all in the arms," he said, and he demonstrated and was instantly high above me, flying homeward, as if he had been born to it.

I was astonished! And the energy of my astonishment was the power I used to lift myself above the prison tower, even as an army of sharpshooters arrived on the beach with their arsenal of crossbows.

Now at this point in the story I have to stop to correct a misconception. It is believed by many people that it was arrogance and pride that attracted me to the sun that day and resulted in my downfall.

No. It was not. It was something altogether different that brought me down.

The reason I faltered is this: I was sick of my father's perfection.

I knew I carried his genes in me, knew my tendency to lose my temper, as well as my weak left eye and my natural suspiciousness all came from him. But the greater gifts, the gifts of the mind, those he hoarded and kept in the dark, locked tower of his superior IQ. And every day I tried to match him, I showed him my drawings, my escape plans, my elaborate and fanciful weapons— and every time he'd laugh at me, point out the obvious flaw in each of them, tell me not to bother myself because the strain would be too much for my inferior intellect and of course he was hatching a foolproof scheme. He'd smile at me, a condescending smile, the smile an animal trainer gives to his clever and limited chimpanzee, the smile I had to endure my entire life long.

I had a right to think myself superior to him! My legs were longer, my eyes clearer, my endurance greater—but I didn't think myself superior.

That tower was cold, always cold. As we flew upward into the blue air above the ocean, I flew straight for the sun. I flew toward what was warm—away from the cold father whose own heart was buried deep within its private labyrinth, inaccessible to all.

Yes, I wanted to show him his invention was flawed and I knew what that flaw was! I could hear him yelling: "You idiot! You fly too high! Don't fly so high!" "Why not?" I shouted back. "The wings! The wax will melt! You'll ruin the wings!"

That's my story.

I tell it to everyone. I'm telling it to you. You don't have to believe me. I suppose, in this space, you have to tell the truth. I'm telling the truth. That's the story of my father and me, before I came to New York.

The wax melted, I fell out of the sky, I crashed into the ocean, I was rescued by fishermen off the coast of Maine, in a coma. I came to, I begged my doctors to go out to sea and find the remains of my beautiful wings. I was pleasantly and firmly rehabilitated.

I pretended to forget my childhood and my brilliant father and my one incredible flight over the sea. But I won't forget.

I cleave to my story, imagining that somewhere nearby my father has again escaped death and is again laughing brilliantly at all of us.

X

Mixed blood is shit.

You're just fuckin' crazy, lady.

Black man with a story about flying! Shit!

Bring it, bitch! Here I am!

I fucked people up.
Blood was like food to me.
Like a god of the night.
Killed a man in the Bronx seven years ago.
Smashed his face clean into the grill of a Lincoln
      Continental
with whitewalls, leather interior, nice shine.
You think I'm sorry?
I'd do it again.
You think I'm afraid?
Don't none of you think I'm going to change.

MARK FERREIRA

This body is a book.
And in my head I can hear
the voices of ancestors:
they've already spoken richly to my genes.
Left their ironies and paradoxes imprinted there.
The voices of my ancestors are nightmare voices,
insistent, untranslatable.

They want me to remember
what part of my body came from the Caribbean.
What part came from Africa. Spain. The Canary Islands.

They ask me: when a nation fights a war
are those battles imprinted on the DNA of the survivors?
What screams are encoded there?
Battle plans, moments of heroism,
a young soldier pissing his pants . . .
which moments become part of the collective memory
to be translated into proteins,
effecting the shape of organs,
thickness of marrow,
location of heart valves,
brain circuits,
patterns of sleep?
What does peace mean in this context?
Don't we tear holes in the wind itself
when we make war?

These are my talkative ghosts:
manifestations of the past,
acting out old patterns, tugging on living flesh,
inept and weak, but there, very there, very right now.
History acts on us like big magnets,
like time's fingertips.
A slave's impulses, a leader's perspiration,
a buried son, the color of a flag—
nothing is wasted. Everything is recycled.

I ask my ancestors:
Who had my face before?
Who shaped my brain?
They laugh.

They know I carry my nation's tragedies with me.
I sing its anthems.
Its coastline mirrors the shape of my back.
I know the laughter and faces of my people
are encoded forever in my deep spaces.

CORDELIA GONZALEZ

On my back, *carajo*, exhausted, couldn't even smoke one fucking cigarette, *esse maricon* doctor and his stupid rules. The baby in the nursery, *gracias a Dios*; I didn't wanna see him. *Dejame quieta*, I know he's my son but, *puñeta, tu sabes*, at that moment, flat on my back, *carajo*, I was grateful for a little rest, maybe watch TV, catch a soap, though it hadda be an American soap, *Days of Our Fucking Lives*, couldn't expect those fucking white boys to let me watch *una telenovela, coño*.

I didn't feel too bad. My fucking body. I could give birth in my sleep, *carajo*. I could have a baby through my nose! I was so good at having *niños*, fuck me, I really couldn't hardly feel him being born. Sixteen friggin' children! *¡Coño!* And no twins! You try it! That's gotta be a world's record! Somebody gotta look that up in a book or something. Get me a door prize of some kind! Sixteen little motherfuckers!

No, I love them, I do, I love every fucking hair on their little fucking heads. Some of my girls, bless them, they saved my life, *Dios mio*. They do a lotta work.

Now another baby! My body! I look like a hippopotamus! My skin don't even feel like skin no more.

So where is he? *¿Donde esta esse maricon?* Not here, at his wife's side, not next to the mother of his sixteen little people, holding her hand, bringing her ice cubes and shit! Just like him— Fernando always found an excuse to miss the birth of his babies. Sixteen kids and he ain't never seen one of the little mother-fuckers being born, *carajo. ¡Que barbaridad!*

So the baby was sleeping. I was resting. My husband was missing in action. And I'm mellow and the phone rang. I said, "What?" No answer. I said, "Who the fuck is this already?" *¡Coño!*

So then she answers. She only says one thing, one sentence: "Well," she says, "you had his baby last night, but I fucked him." Click!

Man, I slammed that fucking telephone so hard! I almost broke my fucking hand! That bitch! That cheap fucking *hija de la puñeta! ¡Me cago en tu madre!* She called me to tell me that: "You had his baby last night, but I fucked him." *Mira que cosa mas* fucked up! *That's* where that *maricon* was last night. With his girlfriend and she calls me to tell me about it! What a class act, huh? *¡Coño!*

The day passed okay after that. After I settled down.

Then the phone rang again. It was my daughter, Lizbeth, the oldest, she's all hysterical, I can't understand her: "*¿Que te pasa, muchacha? ¿Que te pasa?*" She can't settle down and passes the phone to Julian, my oldest boy, *y Julian esta llorando tambien. Ahora me pongo nerviosa.* "*Que paso, carajo,* what's up with you?" Julian *me dice,* "Papi's been hit by a car, Mami."

I don't breathe for a minute. I don't even think.

Julian goes, "He was walking from a friend's house." A friend! From that bitch's house, *essa demonia*! "*¿Tu Papa se murio?*" I ask. "No. But they think he's gonna be paralyzed, Mami." "Paralyzed where?" I ask. "Paralyzed from the waist down," he says. Fernando paralyzed from the waist down . . .

Julian can't talk. He was crying too hard. Surprise. I thought Julian hated his father. Fernando was ruthless with his children and he gave his worst punishments to Lizbeth and Julian. Maybe they were crying from happiness.

KRISTINE NIELSEN

I always came out Wednesday night
to drop my garbage on the curb.
I lived in a quiet neighborhood,
mixed, you know?
Basic Seattle.

Neighbors where Chinese—a doctor
and his wife, a guidance counselor.
Two children.

The wife—
she was a very polite woman, very civil.
She wasn't very tall. She had small shoulders.
Her hair was short and she had a quick, gasping laugh
that made her sound startled and alert.

I didn't know a lot about psychiatry.
Or how the mind works.
I didn't dream much.
But I studied sounds.

Sounds were my source of knowledge of people.
Especially laughs.
I could gauge intelligence levels from a good laugh.
I could analyze prejudices, weaknesses, fears, desires, from any
    kind of laugh,
from any kind of person.

God, if you laughed, I could tell you a little about yourself.
Tell you what kind of day you're having.

God's not laughing today.

Anyway, her laugh was a rich tapestry for me.
I heard her anxieties in her laughter.

I heard the years of stress.
I heard her husband's coldness
and the iron grip he had on her fate.
I heard her disappointments—
the petty racist remarks she'd hear nearly each day at school
    where she worked.
I heard her lamentations in her laugh:
the job is too hard,
she's afraid her children will change,
the neighborhood is getting worse—
this and more were in the sixteenth notes
of her laughter,
the fractured melodies I heard
as clear as symphonies
from the open door of my bedroom,
far from hers,
across the street
whole light-years and a lifetime away.

ALENE DAWSON

My son had his first day of public school Monday.
We had him in a private school in Van Nuys
but it was a little too far away for us,
too expensive, and he'd come home all sad,
saying, "How come there are no
brown faces in my school, Mom?"
So we finally got him into a magnet in Echo Park
—prestigious—
and there was an assembly Monday
and on the stage the principal got up
to talk to the new students and said,
"Okay kids, now don't you be bringing in
no guns to school in your backpacks!
Hear that, children?
I want no guns, no knives,
no chains in your lockers
or in your backpacks
or on your person."
This is the principal!
This is a magnet school in the humanities!
And she says,
"Stay close to the school,
don't wander away from campus.
There have been drive-bys in this area
so don't leave the school grounds!"
I'm thinking, oh my God!
It's getting out of control.
We're at war.
Citizens killing citizens.
We don't need the government to bomb the city.
We do it to ourselves,

taking the knife to cut open the throats
of our own children,
and then when we're out of hand,
when we're too good at that,
the police are brought in,
like an occupying army, you know,
jackboots all polished up,
hardware all glistening,
big robocop shoulders,
nightsticks ripping open the heads
of our little boys—it makes me crazy.
'Cause you know, it's all their fault!
The economy bad?
It's the black kids!
Air pollution?
The black kids did it!
The dollar down against the yen?
You know who to blame! God!
Made me want to take a rock
and hurl it at some politician,
some bozo running for mayor,
any of those quick-tongued hypocrites
assigned to protect the citizens,
'cause, no, I didn't feel protected,
I felt *exposed,* all opened up,
like some criminal was pointing
his Saturday night special at me
and every day I sensed those trigger fingers
out there and I was at the end
of their sights and they were just watching me,
waiting for the right split second
to send a little ounce of screaming steel
into the back of my brain!
God! God! It was not to be believed!

Being a woman in this city,
sometimes, oh my God,
I needed some help!
Especially when my boy went
out that door, you know?
And my imagination has created his killer,
some sweating, over-anxious, rookie cop,
too afraid to piss straight,
slamming into my child at the wrong time,
in the wrong place, 'cause he's thinking,
"Of course, boy's in a gang, it's natural,
they run in packs,
those boys up to no good, you bet.
But what'd you expect?
It's a genetic thing with the black kids,
they're innately less intelligent,
but don't talk to me,
it's already *proven*,
there are *statistics*,
it's testable,
they're naturally more comfortable
with a .45 in their hands
than a volume of Faulkner."
So why the hell not cut the school budget?
Why not send them off
to some genocidal death in the penitentiary?
It's a waste of good American tax money
trying to educate these
unteachable black kids!
Jesus Christ! It's time to build
another super-prison,
you know, with a hundred Nautilus machines
and hot tubs and libraries,
'cause, let's face it,

it's a whole lot nicer on the inside
than the corner of Florence and Normandie.
Going to jail is a good career move!
Oh, God! If I wasn't a peaceful woman
I would've thrown rocks!

Trouble is, I don't think enough people
believe in the multiplicity of God.
Not enough people understand
God's great face has a nose
and eyes of a thousand shapes and sizes
and all of us, down to the last ugliest
and lowest person, we are all the living,
walking *text* of God.
Yes, the life story of God is
written into each one of us:
we are the pages in the book of God's mind.
And if we'd just take the time
we'd be able to read God
in each other's faces,
read the funny lines as well as the lines
of wisdom and healing—
because the Word of God
isn't written in the Bible, no,
the Word of God is written in your mirror
and on your brother's black face
and in your son's blue eyes.

My son. He's the sweetest thing . . .
actually he's a royal pain in the ass
ninety-five percent of the time . . .
but for five sweet percents,
he's my angel of laughter and hope.
My mother is from Guyana.

I was trying to teach my son
a little bit about that heritage,
but it was hard, you know,
that culture's so deep
and I didn't know anything about it.
I told him about South Africa
but, you know, what's that mean?
It's not like the Lakers!
The Lakers you can get up for in the morning!
No, my son's not into Guyana or South Africa.
He's into being a boy.

RENÉ RIVERA

Bueno, I never really made it big as an actor. I'm not ashamed to say that. I worked.

The damn business. Competition killed me. My skin color, my accent, my attitude, my pride.

I could play a great drug addict. Watching myself in dailies, I fucking scared myself.

I mugged, I stabbed, I cheated on women who trusted me, I sold drugs to sixth-grade, inner-city youth. All for NBC.

A line here, five lines there, bit parts, a day player.

Gangsters, hoodlums, angry spicks, pointy black shoes. Drunks, losers, punks, washed-up dreamers, casualties, broken, future-less, fractured men, always dangerous. Men you couldn't trust.

I played a dozen rapists with names like Miguel, Angel, Pedro, Jose, Juan, Miguel—did I say Miguel? In one picture alone, I raped my best friend's wife, my daughter (twice), a little girl who lived in the building, white women of every kind.

On prime time, I delivered pizza, I delivered packages in Manhattan, I snaked clogged toilets, I was a handyman, a mechanic, a grape picker, every kind of janitor in every kind of building, a super super, a petty drug pusher, a drug kingpin—I've been stabbed in the heart, tortured, poisoned, raped by convicts, overdosed eleven times, killed in the electric chair, hit by a subway train, eaten alive by ghetto rats, shot by the cops so often I lost count. I hung myself.

In war pictures I was always the coward. In prison pictures I was always the traitor who ratted on his buddies. In westerns I was the illiterate cook the Indians scalped in the first reel. I've been a buffoon, an asshole, a scapegoat, a pretender, a liar, a misfit. Children and women cheered when I died. Strangers on the street spit at me. And what great dialogue I had: "Take that, bitch!" And: "I don't care if you kill me, sarge, 'cause I'm going straight to hell anyway!" And: "Taste my blade, *cabron!*" Eat your heart out, Lorca!

In horror pictures, I was the asshole who walked into the dark room when the whole audience was going: "Don't go in there, asshole!"

I had eleven agents. Fourteen managers. Countless addresses. I was an angry young actor, then I swallowed anger, tried to mellow out, work with the system, I turned down nothing, I kissed so many asses, I walked the walk, worked out, stopped smoking, laid off the nose candy, went to the right places, shook hands, always looked sharp any time of the day or night, worked on my teeth, got my tattoos burned off, left my attitude, *mira*, at the door, made follow-up calls, wrote notes thanking racist morons for treating me like a bag of come. I turned anger into ambition. I watched young studs doing roles I would never get.

Then I got sick.

Now understand me. I was a middle-aged Latino actor. I was married very young. I had two daughters, and their mother couldn't stand my guts and she took the two girls away and moved to Mexico. I said, "The hell with it," and went out west. Concentrated on the subtleties of playing junkies. I had a fantastic body and once or twice, in the beginning, they called me in to read for Latin stud roles, usually pimps, but twice a male prostitute, a gigolo.

So you understand, I'm in town, separated from the mother of my girls. I'm the Latin stud prospect of the moment—I'm free to sleep with whoever I want—but I can't come out. I come out to nobody. Nobody in the business.

I go where I had to go. I do what I have to do. I don't live with nobody for a long time. I get a fake girlfriend for a little while. I have sex in secret. Nobody knows.

But I get sick anyway. I get it. I fight knowing it, but I get it. And I don't tell nobody.

I get safer. I meet a man. I fall in love. We're "roommates" now. He's decent and pure and a lot younger than me and I tell him, "Babe, you're taking some chances," and he's the home I never had, the island where I find some peace, the wall that surrounds and protects me.

But, you know, I used to drink a lot. And my liver is like melted dogshit. It's a major casualty now that I'm bad sick.

Then I meet a young Latino writer, up and coming, he's all skinny so I nickname him Flaco, and this young man casts me in a role that's like a Latino King Lear—big, the man is big, big appetite, big balls, big language, evil but funny! I never had a part like this and I had told myself, "No plays; I'm only concentrating on the film and TV, and no going out of town!" But this role is the real thing and I say, "Screw it, I'm taking this sucker by the balls and I'm going to be great and show those racist morons what I can really do!"

And I do the play out of town and Flaco and me, we become friends. He gives me hope. He never knows the truth about me, but I'm getting sicker and sicker. My liver, my blood.

I disappear from sight for a year and a half. Flaco doesn't know a thing. I make sure nobody knows.

But one day everything falls apart and I'm in the hospital and suddenly the word is on the street: "Rene's got it. Rene's sick bad." And I'm in a crappy-ass hospital in Hollywood 'cause I'm broke. I didn't want anyone to visit me but they visit and eventually even Flaco visits me towards the end, when I'm bad, really bad and people are getting emergency phone calls saying, "You better see Rene now because you may never see him again."

And one night I'm barely conscious and Flaco comes to visit me. And I know he's there even though I can't talk or open my eyes. My roommate is there and he's trying to make me laugh. He's stroking my face, going, "I know you can hear me, Rene. I know you want to smile. Give me a smile, Rene, come on, I know you can do it, *corazoncito*." And I smile.

And Flaco's standing there trying to talk to me and I don't want him to see me like this. I want him to remember like I was in his play—big, big appetite, big language, evil but funny.

Then one of those pathetic excuses for a doctor comes in and realizes I'm not getting any nourishment because the tube they got running from my arm down to my heart is collapsed and he's got to pull it out again and reinsert a new tube that's not collapsed. So he pulls it out and he's sitting at my bedside and I'm totally unconscious and Flaco is there watching all this and the doctor is trying to insert a new tube in my veins. And the doctor can't get the tube back in my vein again and I'm bleeding all over the place and I can hear that Flaco and my roommate have stopped talking and I know they're just watching this and the doctor is making his pathetic excuses to Flaco and my roommate and finally I'm so damn mad, I try to use all my strength to make a fist and I try to punch the doctor in the face and I'm grimacing and everything in my body wants to hurt this man and I can make my arm move and I take a shot at him and my fist is shaking like the d.t.'s and he's still making his excuses and I try three times to hit him and he tells Flaco he can't get this tube inside me if I keep trying to punch him like this and asks Flaco to hold me down, and I'm so damn mad, and Flaco grabs my left hand and holds it down and I'm struggling against him and my mind is going, "Let me go, let me hit him, let me keep some dignity, what are you doing here anyway, this isn't for you, I'm not a damn show, why don't all of you just leave me alone?" And another voice in my brain is going, "Don't get no blood on you, Flaco, that damn doctor's got twenty layers of plastic but you don't have nothing, let go of me before I bleed on you."

I'm so weak Flaco pushes my arm down so easy.

He's close to my ear and I can hear him breathing. His hands are strong. It's incredible to feel strong skin again, alive blood, a feverless body, strong, I'm nothing against that strength and I almost have to laugh the idea of me punching the doctor, I almost have to laugh.

KIERSTEN VAN HORNE

The first time someone else's tongue enters your mouth.
The first time a child trusts you to carry them to the next room.
The first time you drive safely from Westfield, Massachusetts,
    to San Diego with someone you're in love with.
The first time you watch birth.
The first lines of *Paradise Lost*.
The first time you make a decisive three point shot in a game
    that really counts.
The first time you get the dog to shit outside.
The first time you can read "I love you" in a lover's eyes.
The first time you sleep in after fucking all night long.
The first family reunion without homicidal fantasies.
The first love letter.
The first serious talk about love with your child.
The first time you contemplate suicide and change your mind.
The first hangover.
The first arrest.
The first acquittal.
The first epiphany.
The first time you hear Lorca in Spanish.
The first real friendship with a person of another race.
The first gray hair.
The first time you see Picasso's *Guernica*.
The first time you visit your birthplace.
The first time you hear Lightning Hopkins.

The first visible comet.
The first time you feel attractive and someone calls you "angel."
The first experience with something remotely like a god.
The first recovery after a serious illness.
The first beer with your father.
The first time therapy makes sense.
The first birthday of your first born.
The first time you can't walk and your lover carries you to the
    next room.
The first foul ball you catch in Fenway Park.
The first time you stand alone and you're scared to death and
    you don't change your position.
The first time you're convinced of your mortality and you
    laugh.
The first sunrise after the first death of a parent.
The first time you forgive the unforgivable.
The first time you see the Earth from space.
The first time it is truly obvious that it was better that you had
    lived, at this time, in this world.
The first time you decide every moment of your life should be
    a work of art.
The first time you die and you breathe again and you speak to
    the living.
The first time you realize that it all just might have been okay.

*(The people in the space look up at the silent sky around them.
    They wait.*
    *No revelations come to them. No answers. No giant bolts of
lighting.*
    Just a slow fade to black.)

THE END

36 ASSUMPTIONS ABOUT WRITING PLAYS

Over the years I've had the good fortune to teach writing in a number of schools, from second grade to graduate school. I usually just wing it. But lately I've decided to think about the assumptions I was working under and to write them down. The following is an unscientific, gut-level survey of the assumptions I have about writing plays, in no particular order of importance.

1. Good playwriting is a collaboration between your many selves. The more multiple your personalities, the further, wider, deeper you might be able to go.

2. Theatre is closer to poetry and music than it is to the novel.

3. There's no time limit to writing plays. Think of playwriting as a life-long apprenticeship. Imagine you may have your best ideas on your deathbed.

4. Write plays in order to organize despair and chaos. To live vicariously. To play God. To project an idealized version of

the world. To destroy things you hate in the world and in yourself. To remember and to forget. To lie to yourself. To play. To dance with language. To beautify the landscape. To fight loneliness. To inspire others. To imitate your heroes. To bring back the past and raise the dead. To achieve transcendence of yourself. To fight the powers that be. To sound alarms. To provoke conversation. To engage in the conversation started by great writers in the past. To further evolve the art form. To lose yourself in your fictive world. To make money.

5. Write because you want to show something. To show that the world is shit. To show how fleeting love and happiness are. To show the inner workings of your ego. To show that democracy is in danger. To show how interconnected we are. (Each "To show" is active and must be personal, deeply held, true to you.)

6. Each line of dialogue is like a piece of DNA: potentially containing the entire play and its thesis; potentially telling us the beginning, middle and end of the play.

7. Be prepared to risk your entire reputation every time you write, otherwise it's not worth your audience's time.

8. Embrace your writer's block. It's nature's way of preserving trees and your reputation. Listen to it and try to understand its source. Often writer's block happens because somewhere in your work you've lied to yourself and your subconscious won't let you go any further until you've gone back, erased the lie, stated the truth and started over.

9. Language is a form of entertainment. Beautiful language can be like beautiful music: it can amuse, inspire, mystify, enlighten.

10. Rhythm is key. Use as many sounds and cadences as possible. Think of dialogue as a form of percussive music. You can vary the speed of language, the beats per line, volume, density. You can use silences, fragments, elongated sentences, interruptions, overlapping conversation, physical activity, monologues, nonsense, nonseqiturs, foreign languages.

11. Vary your tone as much as possible. Juxtapose high seriousness with raunchy language with lyrical beauty with violence with dark comedy with awe with eroticism.

12. Action doesn't have to be overt. It can be the steady deepening of the dramatic situation . . . or your characters' steady emotional movements from one emotional/psychological condition to another: ignorance to enlightenment, weakness to strength, illness to wholeness.

13. Invest something truly personal in each of your characters, even if it's something of your worst self.

14. If Realism is as artificial as any other genre, strive to create your own realism. If theatre is a handicraft in which you make one of a kind pieces, then you're in complete control of your fictive universe. What are its physical laws? What's gravity like? What does time do? What are the rules of cause and effect? How do your characters behave in this altered universe?

15. Write from your organs. Write from your eyes, your heart, your liver, your ass—write from your brain last of all.

16. Write from all your senses. Be prepared to design on the page: tell yourself exactly what you see, feel, hear, touch and taste in this world. Never leave design to chance, that includes the design of the cast.

17. Find your tribe. Educate your collaborators. Stick to your people and be faithful to them. Seek aesthetic and emotional compatibility with those you work with. Understand your director's worldview because it will color his/her approach to your work.

18. Strive to be your own genre. Great plays represent the genres created around the author's voice. A Chekhov genre. A Caryl Churchill genre.

19. Strive to create roles that actors you respect would kill to perform.

20. Form follows function. Strive to reflect the content of the play in the form of the play.

21. Use the literalization of metaphor to discuss the inner emotional state of your characters.

22. Don't be afraid to attempt the great themes: death, war, sexuality, identity, fate, God, existence, politics, love.

23. Theatre is the explanation of life to the living. Try to tease apart the conflicting noises of living, and make some kind of pattern and order. It's not so much an explanation of life as it is a recipe for understanding, a blueprint for navigation, a confidante with some answers, enough to guide you and encourage you, but not to dictate to you.

24. Push emotional extremes. Don't be a puritan. Be sexy. Be violent. Be irrational. Be sloppy. Be frightening. Be loud. Be stupid. Be colorful.

25. Ideas may be deeply embedded in the interactions and reactions of your character; they may be in the music and poetry of your form. You have thoughts and you generate ideas constantly. A play ought to embody those thoughts and those thoughts can serve as a unifying energy in your play.

26. A play must be "organized." This is another word for "structure." You organize a meal, your closet, your time—why not your play?

27. Strive to be mysterious, not confusing.

28. Think of information in a play like an IV drip—dispense just enough to keep the body alive, but not too much too soon.

29. Think of writing as a constant battle against the natural inertia of daily language.

30. Write in layers. Have as many things happening in a play in any one moment as possible.

31. Faulkner said the greatest drama is the heart in conflict with itself.

32. Keep your chops up with constant questioning of your own work. React against your work. Be hypercritical. Do in the next work what you aimed for but failed to do in the last work.

33. Listen only to those people who have a vested interest in your future.

34. Character is the embodiment of obsession. A charcter must be stupendously hungry. There is no rest for those characters until they've satisfied their needs.

35. In all your plays be sure to write at least one impossible thing. And don't let your director talk you out of it.

36. A writer cannot live without an authentic voice—the place where you are the most honest, most lyrical, most complete, most creative and new. That's what you're striving to find. But the authentic voice doesn't know how to write, any more than gasoline knows how to drive. But driving is

impossible without fuel and writing is impossible without the heat and strength of your authentic voice. Learning to write well is the stuff of workshops. Learning good habits and practicing hard. But finding your authentic voice as a writer is your business, your journey—a private, lonely, inexact, painful, slow and frustrating voyage. Teachers and mentors can only bring you closer to that voice. With luck and time you'll get there on your own.

JOSÉ RIVERA's plays have been seen throughout the world and have been translated into six languages. He's the recipient of two OBIE Awards for Playwriting (for *Marisol* and *References to Salvador Dalí Make Me Hot*, both produced at The Joseph Papp Public Theater/New York Shakespeare Festival), a Kennedy Center Fund for New American Plays Grant (for *The Street of the Sun*, produced at the Mark Taper Forum), two Joseph Kesselring Award honorable mentions (for *Marisol* and *The Promise*, premiered at the Ensemble Studio Theatre), as well as grants from the NEA, the Rockefeller Foundation and the New York Foundation for the Arts.

Mr. Rivera is the recipient of a Fulbright Arts Fellowship in Playwriting, the Whiting Foundation Writing Award, a McKnight Fellowship, a Berilla Kerr Playwriting Award and the Titan Theatre Company's 2003 Earthshaker Award. His play *The House of Ramon Iglesia* won the FDG/CBS New Play Contest and appeared on the public television series *American Playhouse*. Other premieres include *Cloud Tectonics* (Humana Festival at the Actors Theatre of Louisville), *Each Day Dies with Sleep* (Circle Repertory Company and Berkeley Repertory Theatre), *Sonnets for an Old Century* (Greenway Arts Alliance), *Sueño* (Hartford Stage Company), *Giants Have Us in Their Books* (Magic Theatre, Inc.), *Maricela de la Luz Lights the World* (La Jolla Playhouse) and *Adoration of the Old Woman* (La Jolla Playhouse).

Mr. Rivera studied with Nobel Prize Winner Gabriel García Márquez at the Sundance Institute and was a writer-in-residence at London's Royal Court Theatre. He co-created and produced the critically acclaimed NBC TV series *Eerie, Indiana*. Rivera's teleplay *P.O.W.E.R.: The Eddie Matos Story* (HBO) was nominated for a 1995 Cable Ace Award for Best Children's Program. Half-hour teleplays include "The Haunted Mask" for Fox Television's *Goosebumps* series (pilot), and episodes of *The Brothers Garcia* and *Night Visions*. Feature-length teleplays include *The Jungle Book: Mowgli's Story* for Disney.

He is currently working with Brazilian director Walter Salles (*Central Station*) on three feature films: *The Motorcycle Diaries* (Wildwood and Film Four) featuring Gael García Bernal (*Y Tu Mamá También*), *Martin Sheffield* (Miramax) and *Lucky* (Radar Pictures and Focus Films) and developing an HBO series with director Miguel Arteta (*The Good Girl*). New plays j

and *l*

LAB